Information essentials

for business analysts and project managers
by Igor Arkhipov

MW00914808

< this page intentionally left blank >

Information technology essentials for business analysts and project managers

First published in 2023 by Igor Arkhipov in Melbourne, Australia.
©2023 Igor Arkhipov, https://www.analystscorner.org/

All rights reserved. No part of this book can be reproduced or used in any manner without the written permission of the copyright owner except as permitted by international copyright law (for example fair use for the purposes of study, research, criticism, or review).

Big thanks to Robert Maniaci. Without your help this book would be full of typos and grammatical errors.

ISBN: 9798396566712

Cover illustration by https://www.pexels.com/@pixabay/

Illustrations by Igor Arkhipov unless the source and corresponding license are explicitly stated on the page.

Icons used in illustrations are used under CC BY 3.0 and iconfinder licenses and were originally created by:

- https://www.iconfinder.com/AmethystStudio
- https://www.iconfinder.com/Geotatah
- https://www.iconfinder.com/Flatart
- https://www.iconfinder.com/startupgraphicdesign
- https://www.iconfinder.com/ratch0013

All the trademarks belong to their rightful owners.

IIBA®, the IIBA® logo, BABOK® Guide and Business Analysis Body of Knowledge® are registered trademarks owned by the International Institute of Business Analysis

UML® is a registered trademark of The Object Management Group; BPMN is a trademark of The Object Management Group

TOGAF® is a registered trademark of The Open Group

ITIL® is a registered trademark of AXELOS Limited

I am not associated nor affiliated with the organisations mentioned in the book unless explicitly stated. The name and title of the organisations and standards mentioned in the book are used for educational purposes (i.e. fair use).

< this page intentionally left blank >

Preface

April 2023

This guide was originally written by me as a supporting material to the online course for project delivery professionals (business analysts, project managers, etc.). The book covers the same topics as the online course and can be seen as an alternative to taking the course or as a transcript or substitute to the written conspectus.

This book does not aim to cover all of the topics of IT in depth, but rather to give the reader an overview of the key aspects of IT on a level that will allow them to understand work-related conversations, pick up specific lingo, and gain the basic knowledge required to start adding value in their role or to land their first job.

In my career, I've met a lot of IT delivery professionals: business analysts, project managers, delivery leads, scrum masters, etc. For many of them, IT was not the first job they had. They come from very diverse backgrounds - former bankers, accountants, journalists and even ballet dancers found their passion and career in the thrilling world of information technology. For some people this transition comes easily and naturally; for some it is harder. I have designed this book with these people in mind: to give an overview of the IT world and help you immerse yourselves into a new environment with its own concepts, terminology, and history.

If you are reading this book, you are probably an aspiring business analyst or project manager and you want to apply the core skills of your profession in the world of IT. This book will give you an overview of IT and its key components. It will introduce the key terms and definitions to make it easier for you to navigate the complex world of information technology, develop a better understanding of the domain and land a first job in this area.

It is designed for people with little or no technical background; those intrigued by the world of IT but not committed enough to enrol in a university degree, or similar. As different people may have different prior exposure to the topics of IT, you may find some sections easier or harder to understand. That is ok. If you are enrolled in the companion online course, every time you feel confused, I encourage you to use the course Q&A (which I monitor regularly and reply to students through) or send me a direct message. You can also send me an email. We will solve it all together.

The book is broken down into a few sections following the topics I consider important for any delivery professional to understand to do their job better and be helpful for the technology team they are supporting.

The topics are:

1. What information technology is and where it sits in the enterprise architecture
2. Foundations of software development: lifecycle, key processes, and definitions
3. Foundations of web and networking
4. The topics of automation
5. Data management
6. Cybersecurity
7. IT management

For each section I will also give a list of links to the resources I find useful to study to get a better understanding of the subject matter. Some of them are available for free on the Internet, some must be paid for. I am not affiliated with any of the resources mentioned (except for my own online courses and IIBA® - an organisation that has endorsed some of my training) and I don't benefit from sharing the links; it is completely up to you to follow them or not. I just feel like if there is a source that explains a topic much better than I can, why wouldn't I share it?

I did not name the chapters of the book "chapters", they're lessons. I'm treating this as a learning journey. I've tried to highlight the words that have specific meaning in IT or that have a specific definition in **bold**. Watch out for these and try to remember what they mean; you are very likely to come across these at work a lot.

You will also notice some text highlighted on a grey background

like this.

I use it to break the flow of the conversation and introduce a more in-depth definition or a complementary idea. I hope it helps with comprehension and will not confuse you.

Coming from a business analysis and project management background myself, I understand the value of the core skill set this profession brings. However, having seen way too many examples of otherwise brilliant project managers failing to deliver an IT project because of not understanding how IT is different to other industries, I believe now that subject matter expertise is also important. Of course, one does not need to be a gifted software developer to manage a backlog of requirements for a software development team. But to understand the specifics of the development process and why one way of breaking work down into atomic tasks is better than the other is a crucial skill; it will help you become more useful for your team, gain their trust and respect, and ultimately build a better career.

I hope this book will help you find your way in the wonderful world of information technology.

Sincerely yours,

Igor Arkhipov,
Certified Business Analysis Professional (CBAP®)
Master of Business Informatics (MBI)

Founder and Lead instructor
Analyst's corner
https://www.analystscorner.org/

Table of contents

< this page is intentionally left blank >

Section 1: What is Information Technology?

What is information technology.

How IT helps manage an enterprise.

Concept of cybernetics.

The place of IT in Enterprise Architecture.

< this page is intentionally left blank >

Lesson 1: What is IT?

The modern world is underpinned by technology; unless you run a very rare business and run all the books in an old school analogue format.

In my personal recent experience, I can recall only one company that I know that does not even have a computer on premises. It is an old swimming school founded by a brilliant swimmer turned swimming coach. They have quite a unique teaching method that builds a strong swimming technique. I know this because both my kids go there, and looking at their success, my wife and I decided to enrol as well to improve our swimming skills. But what else surprised me, in addition to the great results, was the total absence of modern IT in sight. They run their bookings, mark attendance and results, etc. in huge books following a somewhat sophisticated method; and they accept payments in cash. There is still a way to pay them via a wire transfer - they do have a website and I did see an older looking computer in the corner of the office - so I guess they still run on some level of IT support, but this is the closest to an IT-free environment I can recall seeing in recent times.

So, unless you are a business like this, you would have a much greater dependency on modern IT. Don't get me wrong, the place was full of tech - specialised equipment to run the pools, etc., but it was just a different sort of tech.

Information technology is different from other types of tech. In a general sense, it concerns general-purpose computing machines. These machines are versatile and could be programmed for various tasks as opposed to purpose-built machines designed to perform a limited scope of functions.

Information technology, or IT for short, is a general term combining all the technology that helps you manage information about your business. This includes tasks such as generation, storage, communication, and the interpretation of that information.

For this to work, we need to consider IT as consisting of a set of components. Often when discussing IT people talk about hardware and software, but what are they?

Hardware is physical equipment and elements of infrastructure that you use directly, or interact with. Hardware will refer to the physical components of a computer system, or a network. It is any part of the computer that we can physically touch because it exists in the real, physical world.

Software is trickier. It can be defined as a collection of instructions, procedures, and documentation that performs different tasks on a computer system. Software does not exist in our physical world, and it is represented by a collection of rules and commands stored in computer memory or on storage devices. Sometimes people would say "a computer program" or "an application" – both are somewhat synonymous to "software".

When you open the top panel of your laptop (the lid) you interact with a hardware component. It triggers the software system to wake up and start showing you the desktop - this is software responding to the command in a set of rules pre-recorded into it.

Out of the combination of hardware and software parts, you can build systems, databases, and networks.

"IT system" is a term that you will hear a lot. And if you work in the IT delivery function, you will likely contribute to the creation of a few of those throughout your career. So, what is it?

An **IT system** stands for an individual application as well as a combination of software and hardware components developed with a specific purpose of processing data in a certain way. When we speak about an individual program, or application, we are talking about an IT system. When you go to your local store, and they use some terminal at the checkout to process your payment and print a receipt - it is also an IT system. When you come to the office and swipe your access card so the door opens - it is also an IT system in action.

For IT systems to work together, or for different parts of an IT system to coordinate, we employ **networks**. These are communication channels that enable and manage an exchange of information between distributed elements of your IT systems or separate systems that are not co-located within one hardware body (known as **nodes**). For example, imagine you have a card reader near the front door to the office building. The central access management system that stores the information about people's access privileges is deployed on a computer in the server room. The privilege information itself needs to be stored in a way that allows it to be structured and easily retrieved to enable quick response to a card swipe. This is where a **database** solution will be used to store the data and provide a way to quickly search through it.

In this scenario, for someone to come into the office, the data read by the card reader needs to be sent to the central system for analysis, and the results of this analysis will be transferred back to the door. Based on the type of response, the door will either open or it will produce an annoying sound of declined access. This interaction happens with the help of networks that connect the parts of the system and enable them to speak to each other.

Modern enterprises have thousands of IT elements - different IT systems consisting of hardware and software components, network components and infrastructure elements that allow those systems to operate and communicate. This requires a lot of management and governance to work together.

Managing your IT involves two important functions:

1. **"Keeping the lights on"** (support & maintenance): Making sure the IT runs in a way that continuously supports the business. You've got some technology that is running, and you've got some people in the business who use this technology and rely on its stability. This is your business operations, and it needs to be supported. The support may include: aspects of administration (e.g. day to day configuration of technology systems to better meet your needs); aspects of end user support (helping users achieve their goals, delivering training, answering their questions and performing some standard operations on their requests); aspects of maintenance (monitoring of the systems, responding to things that go wrong, applying upgrades and patching - "patching" means upgrading the systems to fix known issues and errors). An extension of the support & maintenance function is incident management and resolution. This is a process of responding to a situation when something goes wrong and is either picked up by the monitoring software or is reported by an end user. When this happens, the IT team needs to react to it and either fix the issue or provide a workaround (a temporary solution to enable the usual course of action while a long term fix is being developed).

2. **"On time, on budget"** (project delivery & change management): Continuously improving the IT landscape of the organisation in line with the business expectations and budgetary restrictions. Based on the known demand for IT resources, a plan is built that consists of a backlog of enhancements for the IT systems, expected timelines

and allocated budgets to implement these items within the timelines. These may include things like introducing new pieces of technology, making changes to existing ones, and migrating from old pieces of technology to new ones. All of these are associated with change management - both on a technical and organisational level. Change management allows us to assess if the organisation is ready for the change. On the tech level, this involves ensuring the new solution integrates nicely with the existing landscape and that no information is going to be lost or corrupted during the migration. On the organisational level, this means ensuring the business operations will be uninterrupted during and after the migration, and that people can continue their daily working routines after the change.

Lesson 2: How IT helps manage organisations

Now, we know what IT is. But why is it so popular and why do people invest so much into it? The answer is simple – it helps manage the business. Many years ago, it all started with cybernetics.

Cybernetics is the theory of how information is stored, communicated, and used to direct the state and behaviour of living beings and machines.

There is a whole history of how cybernetics was invented sometime in the middle of the last century and how it evolved over time and received both praise and criticism in the process. We will omit this history lesson and focus on some of the key concepts of cybernetics, because those will allow us to build a bridge between IT systems and the world of business.

Depending on the type of business (and type of IT in question) information technology may serve two purposes:

1. Enabling the operations function
2. Enabling the management function

Enabling the operations is almost self-explanatory. Let's say you run a call centre. The main function (or operation) of your business is to accept phone calls and process them. In the 21st century you will use IT equipment to do it: to accept and route calls. It's simple really: no IT means no operations means the business can't run.

Enabling management is a bit different. It is about helping managers make the right decisions about the direction the enterprise should take. Let's have a look at an example.

Imagine a real-life object, or rather a situation. Say a game of chess. At every moment in time, it is defined by two factors: 1) the situation on the chess board, and 2) whose turn it is. If you know what is happening on the board and who is going to make the next move, you've got the full picture of the state of the game. This is true even if you don't see the actual board or have missed the start of the game.

The same is true for every system - a state of a system can be described through a set of well-defined variables. Having access to these variables enables a manager, or controller, to apply some action to improve the desired variables and outcomes, and to reduce the undesired ones. It is very important to ensure you've selected the right variable to base your judgement on.

A great example of how this works is the thermostat that your air conditioner probably has.

It is defined by just two variables: 1) the current temperature, and 2) the desired temperature. If the temperature falls, it turns the heater on, if it rises, it turns the cooler on.

This is an example of a simple system with a feedback loop. It sets an action, it monitors the results of that action, and it decides how to behave based on these results. This is a feedback loop - something so important in the world of business. It is not enough to have a set of variables that will explain what is happening in your organisation. You need a way to apply correction based on those variables and measure the impact generated by those actions.

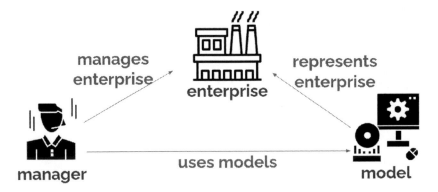

Figure 1 Manager uses models that represent the enterprise to manage it

Business management is akin to that thermostat, they just have more variables to deal with, more complex objectives and sophisticated feedback loops. The objective of management is to apply decision making to drive the business to success. Making decisions should not be a blind exercise. Decisions need to be made based on reliable data. Data that can be provided with the help of IT.

Therefore, you have to model the business, represented as a set of information objects, to management. Based on the status and some quality attributes of those objects, a manager can apply actions to amend the status of the system and to monitor the effect of those actions through the same model.

In other words, for a manager to manage an enterprise, there must be a good model of that enterprise in terms of information objects available to the manager.

What makes a good model? It needs to be reliable, so the data can be trusted. But it also needs to simplify the complex reality to only the items that are important for decision making within the given context.

This brings us to the biggest challenge of building IT systems to help manage businesses - the designer of such a system must identify the critical variables (or objects) to be captured in the system, in order for this set of objects to be enough to make reliable decisions, but not so overly complex that it can't be comprehended by human actors.

The ideas of cybernetics as explained above evolved over time into the theory of system dynamics, activity systems and, eventually, enterprise architecture practices - more about these in the next lesson.

Lesson 3: The place of IT within enterprise architecture

Information technology should never be isolated from the rest of the business. Depending on the type of organisation, IT may play a different role from being supportive in nature to becoming the central part of the business. Regardless of the role, IT is integrated into the organisation and needs to be aligned with how the rest of the business performs.

You may have heard the concept of **vertical silos**. This is something to avoid, and as a delivery professional it is a big part of your job to do it. A vertical silo occurs when different departments, or parts, of the business do not establish productive communication, so all the comms go through escalation lines up to management and then back down to individual contributors in the other team. This slows things down, causes a lot of confusion and builds an "us vs them" mentality between teams and individuals. Unfortunately, IT has a bad reputation for becoming such a silo especially in bigger organisations. With the adoption of modern management techniques such as "Agile software development", "DevOps" and "Flow" some of the communication barriers are broken down. Something to keep in mind when working in IT: do not create silos.

An enterprise architecture (EA) is a conceptual blueprint that defines the structure and operation of organisations. The intent of enterprise architecture is to determine how an organisation can effectively achieve its current and future objectives through its composition, structure, and behaviour.

If we look at any organisation, it may be defined by 2 points of view:

1. How the business is organised, and
2. How the business behaves within this organisation

Let's think about a game of chess again.

The organisation of the game is simple: we've got 2 players, 1 board, and 32 pieces.

But the behaviour is quite complex, and defined by the rules of the game and the roles the participants agree to perform.

The same is true in a business.

A business is organised in different components (teams, units, departments, and divisions), and each one needs to be defined and designed so that it is consistent with the rest of the components. The bigger the enterprise, the more complex an organisation is required to manage it, with some extreme examples seen in huge multinational corporations or governments.

At the same time, just organising people into units will not make the business tick. There also needs to be a set of defined roles for participants (both human and technology) and a set of processes and rules that govern the interactions between these roles.

On an organisational level, it manifests itself as different job positions and descriptions (defining the "roles" for participants) as well as business processes, and workflows, and working instructions (defining the "rules" for the roles to follow).

The same happens on a technology level, as a set of roles people play when interacting with different IT systems and technical workflows between them. For example, a person makes a leave request and their manager needs to approve that request. That's a business process.

Figure 2. A simple conversation between two people may as well be treated as a business process.

In the corresponding IT system automating this process, there will be a role for "an employee" and a role for "a manager", and a workflow allowing the manager to view and approve leave requests based on business logic.

When designing an enterprise as a whole, we need to find a framework and levels of abstraction that allow us to present a holistic picture of that enterprise.

Typically, you will see enterprise architecture slices in the following layers, each one designed and defined separately but in alignment with the others:

1. **Business architecture**: Goals, objectives, organisational structure, and business processes
2. **Information architecture**: Hierarchy of information objects representing the business - on this level of abstraction these can be information objects stored in IT systems as well as physical information storage (think about ledgers, registries, etc.)
3. **IT Systems architecture**: Architecture of information systems and applications managing the information.
4. **Delivery systems architecture and infrastructure**: Architecture of physical components of the architecture including hardware elements and networks.

The deeper we go in this model the higher the level of ownership that the IT department has in it.

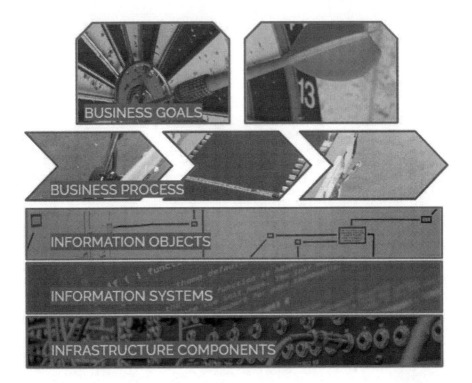

Figure 3. Enterprise architecture levels.

When we go through the topics of this book, we should always keep the bigger picture in our minds: where do we sit within our enterprise architecture. When a change is introduced to a single IT system, we need to be concerned with what the change is about but also with which other aspect/s of the architecture will be affected:

1. Which other systems on the same level of architecture will be affected
2. Which information objects will be affected
3. Which business processes and organisational units will be affected
4. Which infrastructure components are going to be affected

There are formal approaches to building and managing an Enterprise Architecture such as **TOGAF** (the Open Group Architecture Framework). It seems to be the most used framework for enterprise architecture. Still, it receives a lot of criticism in the industry, confirming there is probably no one size fits all approach to Enterprise Architecture.

Useful links for section 1

1. **Understanding the Corporate IT Strategy Game: What You Should Know but Were Never Told**, by **RM Bastien**
    Probably the best overview of the state of play in the IT departments of big organisations. The author explores the dynamics and organisation of corporate IT and reveals quite a few common flaws and pitfalls. An amazing book and I'm looking forward to the second volume coming out soon.

2. **Systems Thinking Renewed**, by **Mr. Graham David Berrisford**
    A great overview and intro into the history behind cybernetics and systems thinking as a prerequisite to understanding the enterprise architecture. The book can get a bit boring and academic at times, but it is extremely useful.

3. **War and Peace and IT**, by **Mark Schwartz**
    The book goes deeper into the topics of digital transformation as it unfolds, but it does also give a good overview of the role IT plays in the modern enterprise making a claim that just as technology is causing a lot of disruption, it is technology that also provides the solutions.

4. **https://www.comptia.org/content/articles/what-is-information-technology**
    CompTIA offers nice resources for IT specialists, including this article. Feel free to click around and read more of their stuff, or maybe even consider a certification.

5. **https://en.wikipedia.org/wiki/Information technology**

I just love Wikipedia and you will see a few more links to it throughout this book. Really, in my humble opinion, it is one of the best things the Internet has given us in recent years. Start with this article and follow the related links or explore the sources to get a great start on all topics.

< this page is intentionally left blank >

Section 2: Foundations of software development

Software development life cycle

Environments

Version control

Pipelines

Integrations and APIs

Services

Solution architecture

Requirements management

Software testing

< this page is intentionally left blank >

Lesson 4: Software Development Life Cycle (SDLC)

On the application level of an enterprise architecture, we've got a whole bunch of applications or Information Systems (IS). Just like for any other tool or asset at the organisation's disposal, one day there is a new need for a new tool, so it is procured or created. At some point the tool is at its peak usefulness and over time the amount of value it brings goes down because the tool becomes less fit for purpose or is replaced by better solutions. So, the information systems need to be created, maintained, and retired in due course. Software Development Life Cycle (SDLC) is a process and a methodology that helps us do this.

> In systems engineering, information systems and software engineering, the **systems development life cycle** (SDLC), also referred to as the application development life cycle, is a process for planning, creating, testing, and deploying an information system.

It is a generic term that may have different definitions depending on the context where it is used, but generally it refers to the fact that all information systems go through a similar set of phases during their life. Similarly to living organisms, they start in some simple state, develop over time, then become less and less powerful (read "less and less useful" in a business context) and eventually proceed to retirement.

Generally, all approaches to SDLC agree on the following conceptual stages:

1. **Ideation/Initiation**
   It all begins when a need for a new system is recognised and proceeds to initial analysis. Usually, it is assessed if the system is viable and feasible to develop and if it is going to be desirable for end users or other beneficiaries.
   At this stage the initial business case will usually be produced, which will assess benefits and costs associated with the proposed solution. Once analysis is concluded and the decision to go ahead is made, the system moves to the next stage (well, I say the "system", but the real system will not appear till stage 3. For now, it is merely a "concept of a system" that exists).

2. **Pre-development**
   This is where the bulk of initial analysis happens: prior to the start of the actual development of the platform. Depending on the project delivery methodology (or how agile the company is going to go) this phase can be short or really long (more about this later). The goal of this phase is to perform an analysis of the requirements for the solution, do the initial solution design, and plan for the resources to deliver it.

3. **Development**
   This is the technical stage of producing programming code for the application and integrating this code with the data sources and infrastructure so it can work in a real-life environment. Typically, you would have separate sub-stages here for development (production of code), integration of the code developed by multiple programmes into a cohesive application, testing if the

application works well, and deploying the solution to a live environment ('What is an environment?', you ask me. We'll talk about it in one of the next lessons. Basically, this phrase means "make the solution available to real users or customers").

4. **Operations and enhancements**

   This is a stage of the lifecycle when the system is available for end users to perform their operations. New development can happen at this stage but the key difference between this stage and the previous one is that the solution already exists here, and we introduce enhancements as changes to the existing systems.

5. **Decommissioning**

   A sad but important stage of the lifecycle when the system is no longer needed. For example, the goal or need for which it was created is no longer relevant for the business, or the system is no longer fit for purpose and needs to be replaced by a better solution.

I've mentioned "agile" before, let's figure out what that means. **Agile software development** is a set of principles and practices for software development that emphasises iterative and incremental development, collaboration between cross-functional teams, and responding to change.

The more agile the company is, the more open to change it is. This means the team will spend less time planning all of the work ahead of time in the pre-development stage of SDLC and will focus on defining just the essentials needed to start the development stage. The rest of the solution specification will happen in parallel with the development, often based on early feedback the team receives from users who see early versions of the final product.

To make it work, Agile software development values breaking down complex software development projects into smaller, more manageable tasks, and delivering pieces of working software early and often, instead of spending months or years developing a complete product. Agile teams deliver small increments of functionality, called iterations or sprints, every few weeks or months, collect feedback, and decide what work to prioritise next based on that feedback.

You may often hear people compare Agile to "**Waterfall**" (the opposite approach), where you define and specify all of the details of the solution prior to development, and then just execute according to the plan. Both ways have pros and cons, but the general consensus in the industry is that Agile has less cons.

Lesson 5: Environments

What does a software product consist of?

At the core of it, there is some logic written using a programming language in a way that allows computers to interpret it.

Imagine you open a browser on your computer and it shows you a webpage. For this to happen, the browser's programming code needs to be written in a way that gives instructions to the computer for how to interpret your (the end user's) commands (e.g., open a web link) and how to interpret the information it receives from other computers (e.g., how to display a webpage).

In addition to having the source code written, a software product needs hardware components and the software it is reliant on to operate. In our case, a web browser requires a computer, e.g., a laptop with an operating system on it.

> The combination of hardware and software required for your software product to run is called **an environment**.

A typical software project will have multiple environments.

It all starts with **a local environment**. A local environment is the setup of a computer that a software developer has. If I am a developer and I want to create a program, I need to set up an environment on my computer so that I can run and test my program as I write the code. If the program needs a particular operating system, I will install it. If it needs a particular hardware setup, I will configure or emulate it. This way, I will create conditions to allow the program to run, so I can see if my code changes produce the desired results.

Having a local environment is good because the developer has full control over it, and it is immediately available. However, often a local computer will be different to the computers where the final product will run, e.g., if we are talking about a web-based product, say a website, the final website will be stored on a server in a data centre which has a different operating system and computing capabilities to the developer's laptop. To ensure the product will work in that setup, a similar server needs to be created that will have some of the key characteristics of the real server. This is often called **a development environment** (or "dev environment") – an environment somewhat close to the real one; an environment where active development and rapid testing are happening.

At the same time, especially in a commercial business, there may be multiple developers producing code for the same project. If they all do it locally on their computers, chances are their code won't work together well. So there needs to be a place where different changes come together and they can be assessed for conflicts. Typically, a separate environment is created for this, called SIT, or **system integration testing** environment.

Speaking of testing, some teams that have a separate testing team decide to also have another environment solely for testing purposes. This is an environment that is usually similar to the integration environment in the way it is set up, but it serves a different purpose – **testing**. So, testers in the team will own it, it will be stable enough in terms of any changes to finish the testing activities, and certify that a particular version of a product is stable and works as expected.

Now that the product is ready to go live, we talk about two more environments. One is usually referred to as the UAT (**user acceptance testing**) environment. It will be as similar to the live environment as possible, and typically more people than just developers and testers will have access to it. This one will be used for business users to try the product before it is live and provide their feedback or formal acceptance of the product (thus the name, "user acceptance").

Finally, **a production environment** (aka "Prod") is an environment that serves real customers and users and processes real data. No jokes or half-baked solutions anymore, production will only hold a well-tested and accepted version of a product. Typically, this one is different to others in a sense that it is better protected in terms of performance and security. You need to make sure your production environment has enough capacity to serve the real-life load of users (you may have just a handful of developers and testers, so the dev environment doesn't need it; but you may have thousands if not millions of actual end users of your product). And also, it has to be secure against cyberthreats and attacks, as you are dealing with real people and their data.

> Preparing an environment for handling real load is called "**hardening**". You harden an environment to be ready for the real world.

As you go from Local to Dev to SIT to Test to UAT to Prod your degree of hardening increases while the rate of change decreases. Typically, dev environments will have more features available on them than the higher environments would have, as every change needs to go through a process and a series of approvals to go up an environment.

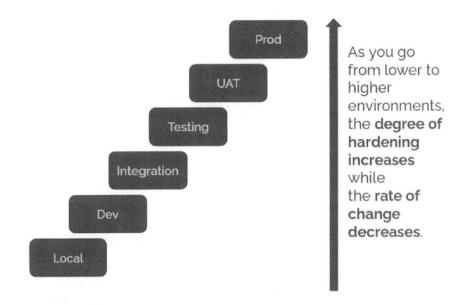

Figure 4. As you move through the environments, the degree of hardening increases while the rate of change decreases.

In order for this to work, you need to have a way to manage different versions of the same software product at the same time and make those versions available in different environments. This brings us to the topic of version control.

Lesson 6: Version control

Imagine you've just started writing software and have written a few lines of code. You save them just like you save any Word document. At the core, programming code is just a list of commands written using text.

Then you make more changes and save them again. And again.

Suddenly you realise your last changes were not needed and you want to revert your system back to how it was before the latest change.

That is what a version control solution allows you to do.

Version control in programming refers to the practice of tracking and managing changes to source code or other types of files. It allows developers to keep a history of changes made to a project and to collaborate with others on the same codebase.

Using a version control system (VCS), developers can create and store different versions of a file or a set of files. This means that they can make changes to the code without losing previous versions and can revert to an earlier version if necessary, or compare the versions to see what changed.

Some popular version control systems used in programming include Git, Mercurial, and Subversion. These systems provide tools for managing code changes, resolving conflicts, and collaborating with others.

Let's look at this diagram.

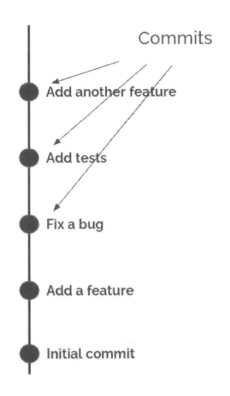

Figure 5. This is what a series of commits will be visualised like in git. A line represents a timeline, a dot represents a version of the codebase associated with a particular commit. Each commit has a human-readable label (but also a unique ID).

Each dot on the diagram is an act of saving a version of a program, or a commit - a version of a file with the code (or multiple files).

A commit is a snapshot of changes made to one or more files in a codebase. When a developer makes changes to the code, they can group those changes together into a commit, which represents a logical unit of work.

A commit typically includes a commit message, which is a brief description of the changes made in that commit. This message is concise but informative and can be used to help other developers understand the purpose and impact of the changes. It can also have a link to a corresponding record in the task management system (if a change is a result of a customer request or a requirement).

Once a commit is made, it becomes part of the project's history, and can be referenced and tracked by other developers who are working on the same solution. Commits are often used to keep track of bug fixes, feature additions, and other changes made to a codebase over time.

A collection of files that contains source code will be called a **repository**, or repo. When you make changes to those files and you are happy with them, you commit them to the repository, effectively creating a version of the repository. The version control system stores it as a separate entity and allows developers to easily go back and forward in time. These versions are immutable, so once created cannot be altered. If a change is needed, it will be created as a new version (commit).

Now, it works well if there is only one developer working on a program. But what if there are multiple developers and they need to work together without interrupting each other? It is something a version control system can help with too.

Version control systems can facilitate collaboration among developers by allowing multiple people to work on the same codebase simultaneously. In this case, people do not directly change the files of the program. Before making any changes, they create a branch - a full copy of the files. This way, any changes they make will not affect the original files until it is time to combine them.

Let's imagine Developer 1 and Developer 2 make their branches and start creating their commits into them. Once they are happy, they need to merge the branches back into the main version.

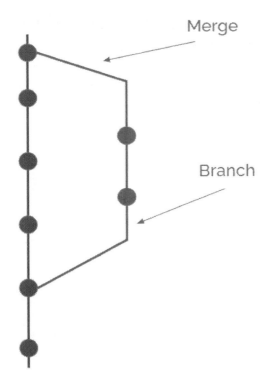

Merge

Branch

Figure 6. This is how a branch will look like as visualised in git. It represents a separate timeline of an alternative version of the codebase that exists from the moment it has been created ("forked" from the main branch) till the moment it is merged back.

Each branch can be associated with an environment. When a developer is working on a feature, they create a branch that they work on locally. But for multiple people to work on the same codebase, that code needs to be stored in a shared location that everyone can access. So when a developer creates a new branch for themselves, they create a copy of the codebase on their local computer. Once they are ready, they need to send the changes to a shared version of the code and merge them with the original branch. There are two ways of doing this:

1. **Push**. Once ready, a developer tells the program to send all their changes back to the main branch. This is a quick and easy way of doing it, but it is risky. What if the two developers made a change to the same file or same line of code? Then the change that is pushed last will override previous changes and the work will be lost (well, not lost per se... but still buried in the older versions of the code, making it harder to retrieve, but also not available to the users).
2. **Pull request.** This is an alternative way of sending your changes back. A developer will request a pull. This means that changes will not be automatically applied to the original files. Instead, the system will wait for someone to review the changes, resolve any conflicts, and accept them. This way, in a team of multiple developers there are always at least two people reviewing the changes before they are merged - and if any conflicts are identified (e.g., a change is proposed for a file that was changed by another developer after the first one created their branch) they can be identified and resolved.

This ability to create branches out of static text files is the feature that allows us to maintain multiple environments, as we discussed in the previous lesson.

Each environment will be associated with a branch of code. And there will be a workflow (or a set of agreements) in the development team on how the code can go from one environment to another. Usually, it is quite a linear process - so the changes must go through all the environments in a particular order.

The way different branches are organised and versions of software move from one branch to another is called a **branching strategy**. Each team may define its own strategy, but there are a few commonly used ones. Gitflow, GitHub flow, Gitlab flow are examples of common branching strategies. You can easily google them online.

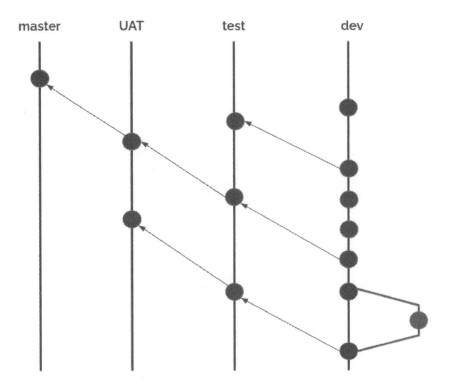

Figure 7. Each environment is associated with a branch of code.

A change (for example a new featured development) starts in the development branch. Once enough features are accumulated in that branch, they will be merged into the testing environment. Once enough features are tested, they will be merged into UAT, and when UAT is complete, the code will be merged into the production environment to make it available for end users. Judging by the amount of commits in every branch you can see that lower environments see smaller and more often changes. These are individual changes, bug fixes, contributions, etc. When there is enough change accumulated, it will be committed to the branch associated with a higher environment.

We need to understand that this process is just managing **versions of the source code** used for a piece of software in an environment. This is not the process that manages versions of the product itself. For an actual change to occur on a product, there is a whole separate process that converts the source code into working executable software. Each environment needs to pick the proper branch and use it to compile a solution based on the version of programming code available in that environment.

Lesson 7: Pipelines

Developers use programming to build products but also to automate boring and tedious tasks, as well as highly important tasks (so there is no human error in the process). Deploying software into an environment is one such task.

How does programming code become working software?

The code written in a human readable language needs to be converted into machine executable code. We call it **compilation of the code**.

The code needs to be compiled to become a working application. When it is compiled, the operating system can start executing the application.

The process of compiling creates all needed executable files, libraries, and packages that the software will use. Many popular programming languages, for example C++ and C# require this process.

Note: not all programming languages require compiling to run. Some languages are **interpreted** rather than compiled, which means the interpretation of human readable language into machine code happens at the time of execution and not prior to it. This requires installation of a special interpreter that will do the job for you. Python and JavaScript are examples of such languages. However, even for interpreted languages there may be steps to convert the source code into an executable application, e.g., to prepare data files.

Once the files for the application to run are created, we can conduct a level of testing to ensure the software has compiled correctly; and then deploy it to an environment, or in other words get it **installed**. When we say installed, we mean all the files are un-archived and placed in the necessary directories, any configurations are performed so the software can run, and all included changes are available to users. At the same time, there are instances when our updated code will mean we need to make changes to the context of the program, e.g., databases that store data for our application (more on databases later).

Finally, we need to test that the application is in fact available and is running as expected.

So, when we update the source code associated with a particular environment, say with UAT, we need to make sure the code is compiled (or otherwise processed) first, and that after that the resulting file, or set of files, are installed on a server.

All these steps can happen by hand: someone (a system admin) can manually move the files, make changes, perform installation steps, update databases, and do initial verification.

But often those steps are repeatable and can be automated. This is when a **deployment pipeline** comes into play. A pipeline (also known as "DevOps pipeline" or "CI/CD pipeline") will be a set of commands that specialised software performs based on a manual or automated trigger, e.g., merging code to a particular branch can be a trigger to start the deployment process that will ensure that the code is converted into executable files, that are then installed on the correct server with the correct access rights, and checked that they run as expected. This speeds up the development process and reduces the chances for human error.

A deployment pipeline is a term often found in the context of CI/CD. CI/CD stands for **Continuous Integration and Continuous Deployment** (or Continuous Delivery). It is a set of software development practices that involve automating the building, testing, and deployment of software applications, ensuring faster and more reliable delivery of high-quality software.

Continuous Integration (CI) is the practice of merging code changes from multiple developers into a shared repository and automatically building and testing the application to catch and fix any issues early in the development process. This helps identify and resolve integration conflicts, coding errors, and other issues quickly, reducing the risk of introducing bugs into the software.

Continuous Deployment (CD) is the practice of automatically deploying the built and tested software to specified environments after passing through the CI process. This helps ensure that the latest version of the software is always available for testing, user feedback, and deployment to production, resulting in more frequent and faster releases.

Both practices are a big part of **DevOps** culture. This culture promotes collaboration, communication, and automation between software development (Dev) and IT operations (Ops) teams. DevOps aims to streamline the software development and deployment process, allowing organisations to deliver high-quality software faster and more reliably.

Lesson 8: Integrations and APIs

When creating a programming solution, it is not always enough to create one application or one program. Multiple programs may need to collaborate and exchange information.

In a simple example, imagine you've got a list of products for your online store, and you have several applications that help you manage the store operations. One application represents the retail sales part of the business: every time a product is sold, the sales process is happening in that system. Another application represents your order delivery department: it manages the delivery of products to customers.

The delivery application needs to know the details of the order to print delivery labels and dispatch deliveries.

One way of doing this is by allowing both systems to access a common data storage. For example, your sales system maintains a spreadsheet file (or a more complicated data structure) that contains all of the orders. Every time an order is created, it is added to the file. The delivery system also has access to the same file, so when a new line is added, it can process this line and start executing the order.

This may work, but if you have any previous experience in IT, you will start frowning at this point. It is a bad practice, and it has a lot of limitations. What if both systems need to make updates simultaneously? What if one system accidentally rewrites the file and breaks it for another system? What if someone else accesses the file and makes malicious changes?

All these points call for a better solution.

Implementing an API - an **application programming interface** - is a way to solve these problems. An API describes the rules of how one system can communicate with another one.

Usually, an API is associated with an **endpoint** - an IP address or a URL that one system may use to send data to another system. If you don't know what an IP or a URL is and how they work, don't worry, we'll cover them later. Just remember they are similar to the address of a website; it's just that instead of a webpage, the address will return something different, such as a data object or a confirmation of accepting a request.

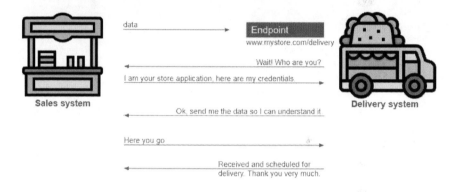

Figure 8. A somewhat silly yet realistic depiction of how an API works.

Second, in addition to having an endpoint, an API will usually have a certain means of authentication. We will talk about this in more details when discussing security, but, in a nutshell, it is a way to ensure that the system sending data to an API is a legit system. You don't want a criminal to be able to send order requests to your delivery system bypassing sales.

Finally, an API will have a specification for the type of data it expects and the format for this data, e.g., for an order management system, an API may expect the following data:

```json
{
    "order_id": 123,
    "products":
    [
        {
            "product_id": 1,
            "quantity": 2
        },
        {
            "product_id": 2,
            "quantity": 4
        }
    ],
    "address": "123 high street",
    "email": "name @example.com"
}
```

The above is a JSON file format.

JSON is a format for text documents that ensures data is structured and can thus be processed by a computer system.

It consists of key-value pairs. For every piece of meaningful data you want to store, it will be associated with a corresponding name for that value. In the example above, a delivery address has a label (or a key) – "address" – and a value for that key – "123 high street". This way the other system will know that when it needs to know the delivery address for a particular order, it needs to pick a value from this particular key.

JSON supports having individual values associated with a key, such as the order id or address here, but it can also have lists of values. A list means you've got multiple values associated with one key. In our example, we have multiple products in one order; this is described as a list. Lists are enclosed in square brackets [like this]. A list may have a collection of simple values, but in our example, it is a bit trickier. Our list contains multiple complex items called objects.

An object works like a dictionary combining a few keys and values together. If you know which key you need, you can get the value associated with it. Just like in a dictionary, if you know the word you are looking for you can read its definition (ok, that may not be the best analogy, but I can't come up with a better one). It is an element that consists of multiple keys combined into one logical entity. Look how we've got a product ID and a quantity for each element in the "products" list. Each item in that list is an object. An object will be surrounded by curly brackets {like this}.

JSON doesn't have to be the format for data exchange via an API, but it is one of the most popular formats. You may also encounter formats such as XML or YAML for data exchange, as well as more rare or even bespoke formats. In any case, the system you are sending a request to will expect a particular data structure and format to be able to process the request.

At the same time, the system sending the request will also expect a strictly defined answer, for example a status code or an error message.

For any API, the developers (if they are reasonable and skilled) will produce an **API specification** that will explain what types of requests an API supports, what the format and possible values for that request are, and what the format and expected values for any type of response should be.

Having these API specifications (sometimes called an API contract) is an important step when designing a cross system interaction. It allows multiple teams to develop their own systems simultaneously, without waiting for the other party to finish their work.

Lesson 9: Services

Now that we know what an API is, we can talk about services.

A service is an application with a defined purpose and a specified API, which is used by other applications.

In our example of an online store, to deliver an item we need to make sure the address entered by the person is valid. We could of course build our own complicated address validation system, but it would probably be overkill. Other companies have already done it for us. For example, a postal service or a delivery partner may have a solution for it. Or Google will have a way to validate addresses via their Google Maps. All we need to do is integrate with their API so we can use a service from them.

The benefits of services architecture are that instead of building one huge monolithic software that does everything, we build a collection of smaller elements with defined purposes. This allows us to replace elements quickly if we need to, switch them on and off based on business needs or an emergency, and even use different technology stacks for each element, e.g., using a faster but sophisticated technology to process complex search requests while using a more user-friendly solution for elements that require a lot of human interactions.

An approach to designing solutions based on services is called a **service-oriented architecture**.

People love service-oriented architecture because it brings a lot of benefits, including:

1. Scalability: Services can be scaled up or down easily based on demand, allowing businesses to accommodate

changing user requirements without having to modify their entire infrastructure.

2. Resilience: Services can be designed with high availability and fault tolerance, making them more resilient to failures, outages, and other disruptions.
3. Modularity: Services are designed to be modular, meaning that they can be developed, tested, and deployed independently of each other. This makes it easier to add new features, fix bugs, and make other changes without disrupting the entire system.
4. Reusability: Services can be designed to be reusable, meaning they can be used across different applications and systems. This reduces development time and costs, and allows organisations to leverage existing services rather than building everything from scratch.
5. Security: Services can be designed with security in mind, making it easier to enforce access controls, implement authentication and authorization mechanisms, and secure data in transit and at rest (more on security later in the book).
6. Interoperability: Services can be designed to be interoperable, meaning that they can work with other services, applications, and systems. This makes it easier to integrate new and existing systems, and to exchange data and information between them.

Overall, the use of services in IT provides many benefits that can help organisations to be more agile, efficient, and effective in delivering solutions to their users and customers.

To use or not to use services is one of the architectural decisions that the IT team needs to make. In the next lesson we will discuss what solution architecture is.

Lesson 10: Solution architecture

Solution architecture (SA) is an architectural description of a specific solution.

> **Solution architecture** is the process of designing and defining the technical architecture of a software system or application. It involves analysing and understanding the requirements of a particular problem or project, and then designing and implementing an appropriate solution to meet those requirements.

Imagine you need to build something simple, like a mobile application that helps you keep notes. Even a simple app like this will require quite a few architectural decisions, which may impact the ability of the app to address your needs - today and in the future.

One architectural question is: where do we need to store the notes? Once you enter the note on your phone, it needs to be saved. A simple solution is to save it on the device itself. It's simple and does not require an Internet connection. However, in the future you may need to synchronise your notes across devices, e.g. between your phone and tablet or between two phones. In this case, storing notes locally will become a problem as the notes won't be available for the other device to show. Therefore, it is better to implement a step to synchronise them with a remote server every time you save a note. The server can then be used to send notes to other devices you own. Suddenly, our solution architecture has more elements: the mobile device itself + the remote server.

However, the Internet is not always available. Imagine the network is down or you are out of mobile coverage. You will need a temporary solution to store notes locally while waiting for the network, so they can be queued for synchronisation and get synced when the device is back online. This is another component to our solution – a synchronisation queue.

For the sync process to be secure and reliable, we need to implement some authentication methods to make sure the notes are sent to the right device and not to someone else. We need to implement an authentication service that will protect the data from being exposed to an unauthorised user.... and so on. More and more architectural decisions will arise.

A **solution architect** will design the solution in terms of solution components and interactions between them, as well as selecting the technology elements used to implement those components.

Depending on the project needs, you may face a different level of fidelity for the solution architecture. A **conceptual architecture diagram** is almost a sketch; it is very basic and abstract. The diagram will be lightly technical and will only highlight key components or large building blocks of the solution. It will also show the existence of relationships between those components without the details of the interactions. You may say that it depicts the strategy of the solution within a context. It is valuable because it forms the basis for a viable solution implementation, and it is a way to get an initial agreement of the direction the solution will go.

Logical architecture is the next step from a conceptual one. On this level, you detail specifics interactions between building blocks, such as: what type of data is there, which order the data should flow, and which direction it should go in. This level of abstraction helps instruct the software development teams on how to implement the solution. But this level of architecture is produced without reference to code, coding, or related implementation techniques. It forms the basis for more detailed solution design and documents the system for troubleshooting, upgrades, and even potential future migrations. It is a map of the future state landscape.

Integration architecture provides a specification for multiple systems to integrate. If you remember what an API is (i.e. a set of rules for how systems interact and communicate), you know what integration architecture is all about. This step provides detailed instructions on how to build APIs for different systems so they are aligned, and will work together once built. This step is one step closer to implementation specifics; it is prescriptive for implementation and tells the developers what to build and how.

Application architecture further defines the black boxes of individual systems or components. On previous levels we were only worried about how different components work together, now is the time to see how each component is organised from within to support the desired observable behaviour. It explains which libraries to use, which classes to build, which coding practices and standards to follow, etc.

Finally, **physical architecture** explains how all this software is going to be deployed on physical components – servers and networks.

As you can see, each level of solution architecture describes how the solution will implement the requirements once it is built, but focuses on a different aspect of the solution at a different level of abstraction.

Lesson 11: Requirements development

A software system cannot be built without someone thinking about what they want their product to do.

The answer to this question is hidden in a set of requirements for a piece of software. It is fair to say that the software development process starts not when the first line of code is written, but when the business needs are understood and recorded as requirements. In the previous example of synchronisation, if we know there is a requirement to sync notes across devices, we will design a solution architecture that supports it. If a requirement like this is not uncovered or does not apply, our solution may be simpler or just different.

So how do we make sure we've uncovered all of the requirements? We follow a structured process to discuss and document all of the different types of requirements.

Typically, when working on requirements for a tech solution we deal with 4 levels of requirements:

Business requirements tell us what we want to achieve with this solution. They are typically described as goals and target values for particular business metrics, e.g., "to increase conversion rate by 2%", "to increase revenue from mobile channel by 10%", "to decrease average processing time by 2 minutes", and so on. These types of requirements inform the business case and are used to determine if the project is a success after it is implemented.

Stakeholder requirements are developed in response to business requirements: these are the needs of individual end user groups, which, when satisfied, will help achieve business objectives. These could include requirements from end users, administrators of the solution, technical support personnel - all of the people who are going to interact with the solution or benefit from it.

Solution requirements are the detailed descriptions of expected features of the solution. For example, you may have a stakeholder requirement to enable reporting of the amount of orders processed by the system. This can be detailed as a set of solution requirements:

1. To have a button in the user interface to generate a report
2. To include dates, number of orders, and total value of orders for each date
3. To send the report as an email to the person requesting the report
4. To store the fact that the report was generated in the system logs

This is a great example of a **functional requirement** – a requirement that explains how an element of a solution should function in response to an event or a trigger.

Some other requirements that we consider on the solution level are **non-functional requirements** - the types of requirements that describe the quality attributes of the solution. They don't answer the question of "what the solution should do", but rather "how well a solution should do it".

Examples of non-functional requirements might be requirements for performance (how fast a solution should process requests), or scalability (how many users the solution should service at the same time), or security, etc. These non-functional requirements will inform many architecture decisions for the solution.

Finally, **transition requirements.** Often when a new technology solution is implemented, it is introduced to replace an existing system or solution. As a result, time is spent to determine the need to migrate data, to recreate accounts, to train users, etc. These types of requirements are called transition requirements: the requirements for how the organisation will transition to the new technology platform.

Business requirements	
Stakeholder requirements	
Solution requirements: functional	Solution requirements: non-functional
Transition requirements	

Figure 9. Levels of requirements

For a project delivery professional, being on top of requirements is one of the most crucial tasks. It will help you manage the scope of the solution and adequately estimate the effort and resources needed to deliver it.

Lesson 12: Software testing practices

Once a piece of solution is done, it needs to be tested to ensure it is good enough to be released to the live environment. Typically, a project will have a few **quality gates** – or main testing checkpoints – to see if the project is on track and of good quality.

Each individual requirement will be implemented in a single feature or a set of features in the solution. A **feature** is a collection of functionality or business logic, e.g., a report generation process can be considered a feature, or a product listing for an ecommerce website can be a feature.

Once a feature is developed, it needs to go through functional testing. Functional testing is effectively an audit that confirms that the feature implements all aspects of a requirement and works as planned.

Once the individual features are tested and pass the test, we can schedule an **end-to-end test**. This is a test that verifies that the solution as a whole performs as expected, that different features work together well, and that different integrated systems or services perform as planned.

Every time we introduce a change to the program there is always a risk that something that used to work before will be broken. To avoid this risk, we run **regression testing**. This is a re-test of functionality that has already passed a level of testing before. The goal is to ensure the functionality is not broken after a new change is introduced.

Next, we can perform a version of **user acceptance testing**. Unlike previous tests, this one is not performed by a professional tester, but rather a potential end user of the solution, someone with subject matter expertise and an opinion of what they need and want from the solution.

And finally, we can perform **non-functional testing**. This is used to check that the solution as a whole meets our quality attributes. Remember the non-functional requirements from the previous lesson (performance, security, etc.)? Non-functional testing aims to validate that the solution satisfies them.

An example of a non-functional test is a **performance test.** To run it, a tester will set up a specialised program to emulate a high load of user requests to our application, so that the tester can monitor its performance. These types of tests help confirm that the solution can withhold an expected load, but can also help us understand what the maximum load that a solution can handle is before breaking or becoming unresponsible due to being overloaded. Think about gambling websites on the night of a big game; or government websites on the deadline for tax returns; or lottery websites on the day of jackpot; or popular retailer websites on the day of a massive sale event – these are all scenarios when we have to ensure performance is sufficient to service a massive spike in user demand.

Non-functional testing should be performed against each category of non-functional requirements, including, but not limited to, performance, security, usability, scalability, recoverability, etc.

Some of these tests can be done manually. This means a person will follow a script to test that the solution works according to its specifications. Some of the tests, however, can be automated, or semi-manual. For example, for a simple scenario of being able to log in with different credentials, a tester can write a program that will mimic a real user and interact with the solution instead of a human. Such a test is faster to execute but it may generate some false negative results. A false negative is a result that indicates failure (the solution does not meet expected criteria), but in reality, there is no error or defect, just an expected change that the automated test was not tailored for. That is why all errors reported by automated tests should be reviewed by a human. Still, automation saves a lot of time and helps with repetitive tasks such as regression testing.

Some types of tests cannot be run manually, such as performance tests. To emulate thousands of users using a system at the same time we need to use automation tools.

You may ask whose job it is to perform these tests. Well, the answer is "it depends".

Modern development practices put more emphasis on the need for developers to test their own products, with practices like Test Driven Development mandating that a level of testing happens prior to a product leaving a developer's hands.

Test-driven development (TDD) is a software development process where tests are written before any functional code. The process works as following:

1. Understand the requirement and write a test: The developer writes an automated test case that checks that the solution behaves as expected by the requirement, e.g., if you have a requirement to convert a suburb name into a postcode, the test will send a list of suburb names to the application and will expect a list

of corresponding postcodes back. The test, when executed, will obviously fail because the functionality does not yet exist.

2. Write the code to pass the test: The developer writes the code needed to pass the test. This code may be incomplete, but it should be enough to satisfy the requirements of the test.

3. Run the test: The developer runs the test and it starts to pass (unless there is a bug in the code, at which point the developer keeps working on the code until the test passes).

4. Refactor the code as needed: From now on the developer may make changes to the code to improve its quality without changing its behaviour (this is called **refactoring**) - and the automated test will indicate if the behaviour is indeed the same.

People do TDD because it ensures that the code meets the requirements of the test at the time of writing the code and in the future. This way it reduces the number of bugs in the code, since the code is tested thoroughly throughout the development process.

The concept of a testing pyramid can help you understand the ownership of testing better.

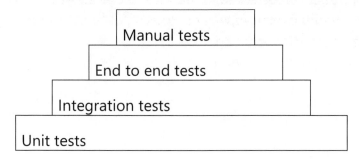

Figure 10. Testing pyramid.

At the bottom of the testing pyramid are **unit tests**. Unit tests are a big part of test-driven development. The idea is that for every piece of logic (every function in the programming code) a developer needs to write a corresponding testing function, so that the code that the developer produces tests itself on the lowest level. This helps to establish a foundational level of quality effectively ensuring the codebase is non-contradictory to itself, so that some functions in the code do not break the functionality of other functions. This level of testing is always owned by the developer writing the code, but it does not guarantee that the product as a whole will work. It's like making sure that all the components of the bicycle are functional – pedals, breaks, gears, etc. - but without actually taking the bicycle for a ride; if the components are not assembled properly, it still won't work. Unit tests won't pick this up.

Integration tests - the next level of testing - make sure different components of the solution work together as expected. Integration tests tend to be automated or semi-automated and their goal is to make sure that all of the APIs work as expected. Integration tests can be owned by developers or specialist testers on the team.

End to end (E2E) tests or **User interface (UI) tests** are the tests performed from the perspective of a potential user. Functional, regression, and UAT tests mentioned above would usually be performed on the E2E level to be accepted. This is where a specialist tester would normally take over and take ownership. These tests can be both automated or manual, and often it is a combination of both.

Useful links for section 2

Alright folks, this is going to be a long list. Pick and choose ;)

1. **Beginning Software Engineering**, by **Rod Stephens**
   A book that explains software engineering methodologies and techniques without jargon and assuming you have no previous programming, development, or management experience. A great entry point into the depth of software engineering and development.

2. **Modern Software Engineering: Doing What Works to Build Better Software Faster**, by **David Farley**
   Another book that takes a closer look at the software engineering practice. It emphasises that software engineering is much more than merely producing code - it is a practice that seeks ways to add more value through software solutions and unlocks creative problem solving processes.

3. **https://en.wikipedia.org/wiki/Systems_development_life_cycle**
   As usual, Wiki offers a nice intro into a few of the topics covered here. Read the articles, follow the links and explore the cited resources.

4. **https://www.atlassian.com/git/tutorials/what-is-version-control**
   An online and free to use guide to Git by Atlassian (a company that has created quite a few tools for software development and team collaboration, including task managers, knowledge bases, automation systems, etc.). A great and easy to understand guide. If you want to learn a bit more about how version control using Git works, it is an amazing start.

5. https://www.mulesoft.com/resources/api/what-is-an-api

   A nice and short video explaining how APIs work created by MuleSoft - a company specialising in API management.

6. https://aws.amazon.com/what-is/service-oriented-architecture

   https://www.ibm.com/au-en/topics/soa

   Pretty much any big IT service provider has an article on their website explaining what a Service-Oriented Architecture is and how their company can help you build one. Take these with a grain of salt, but they do explain the concept. Here are two examples by Amazon and by IBM.

7. **Software Requirements**, by **Karl Wiegers**, **Joy Beatty**

   Probably the best (or one of the best for sure) books on requirements engineering and management.

8. https://medium.com/analysts-corner/4-types-of-requirements-you-will-use-on-all-projects-db6767afc61e?sk=2cb68950dee0e5644425a0d8fae3f05a

   I wrote this article some time ago to explain the four levels of requirements. It echoes what we covered in this section but explains it a little bit differently.

9. https://www.ibm.com/au-en/topics/software-testing

   An overview of testing practices with some case studies by IBM.

10. https://www.istqb.org/

    This company is a great source of knowledge and professional certification for software testers. Explore their resources and learning paths if you want to learn more about testing.

11. https://en.wikipedia.org/wiki/Software_testing

    A very comprehensive wiki article on testing. As always, explore the links and sources.

12. https://www.json.org/

This is a formal specification of JSON format. It is a bit technical and heavy to read, so feel free to just google how to use it instead of reading the spec. But if you need all of the details, use this link.

< this page is intentionally left blank >

Section 3: Foundations of web and networking

Networking

Overview of the OSI model

The Internet

< this page is intentionally left blank >

Lesson 13: Networking

In the previous section we spoke about writing computer programs, using environments to host them, and letting applications talk to each other over APIs.

However, none of this would be possible if computers and other machines did not have ways to send information to each other when they are not connected.

Networking is a specific branch of information technology and is one of the fastest-growing areas of IT. It involves the processes of building, using and maintaining computer networks – including hardware, software and protocols – so that multiple computing devices can share data.

This is what networking is all about. For one application to send a message to another application, they need to be running on computers that have network access to each other; they could be connected physically by an actual set of wires or by antennas using radio waves.

So, how do computers talk to each other?

Imagine you work in an office, and you have multiple laptops. You want these laptops to share information between them, so you need to create a network between them using cables or Wi-Fi. Effectively, all the computers in your network will get connected through some central location, otherwise known as a **switch**.

Once this is done, each computer will be connected using its networking interface - a special card or chip designed to handle network connections. This card will have a unique address – called a **MAC address** - that uniquely identifies the device.

A **media access control address** (MAC address) is a unique identifier assigned to a network interface controller (NIC) for use as a network address in communications.

Figure 11. What a network interface controller may look like.
Source:
https://en.wikipedia.org/wiki/Network_interface_controller#/media/File:ForeRunnerLE
_25_ATM_Network_Interface_(1).jpg CC BY-SA 3.0

There are no two network interface cards in the entire world with the same MAC address, so if we know the MAC address of the destination computer and we are on the same network as that computer, we can send a targeted message to it using its MAC address as a unique identifier.

However, this is not how the Internet works. The problem is that there are billions of devices that are not connected directly, so you can't really reach the device if you only know its MAC address. In fact, in most cases you don't know the MAC; this is where an IP address comes in handy.

> An **Internet Protocol address** (IP address) is a numerical label (for example 192.0.2.1) that is associated with a device connected to a network using the Internet Protocol for communication.

Imagine you have a local network set up in your office. Next to your office is the office of another company. They also have their own local network. Now imagine you need to send them a message. Because you sit on different networks, you can't directly send a message from your computer to their computer. Instead, you need to send it to a device in your local network that has access to the Internet (the higher-level network of networks). Usually, this device is a **router**. A router uses an IP address to first locate the network where the destination computer sits, and then to instruct the local switch within that network to locate the physical address associated with the IP address that you know. It may get a bit confusing but hang in there and we'll figure out how this works.

An IP address consists of two parts - **network** and **host**.

The **Network part** helps locate the network where your message will go, and the **host part** identifies an object (a computer or another device, such as a printer or router) within that network. IP addresses are normally expressed in dotted-decimal format, with four numbers separated by periods.

If you've got Wi-Fi at home, your computer probably has an IP address of something like **192.168.0.3**.

To find out what your IP is, first you need to open the command line on your device. Search for "cmd" on Windows, or open "Terminal" on Mac. If you are running linux, you probably don't need this book anyway ;) Then type the following command "ipconfig" without the quotation marks. You will see something like this:

```
Wireless LAN adapter Wi-Fi:

    Connection-specific DNS Suffix  . : home
    Link-local IPv6 Address . . . . . : fe80::b954:38a7:a6ff:4982%10
    IPv4 Address. . . . . . . . . . . : 192.168.0.11
    Subnet Mask . . . . . . . . . . . : 255.255.255.0
    Default Gateway . . . . . . . . . : 192.168.0.1
```

Figure 12. Example of ipconfig command result on a Windows laptop

It shows the IP address associated with your device on your network.

"IPv4 Address" here corresponds to your IP address within your local network.

Default gateway corresponds to the IP address of a device inside your local network that has access to the global network (e.g., your router). Every time you interact with the Internet, the messages will go via that device.

Subnet Mask shows how many symbols of your IP address are reserved for the Network and Host parts. If you see "255", you know that part of IP is the network part. On the screenshot above according to the subnet mask, **192.168.0** is the network, and **11** is the host. So basically, my laptop is the device number 11 on my home Wi-Fi network.

However, if you go to Google and ask "what is my IP address" you will see something else, e.g., **115.23.19.158**. This is an indication that Google (and any other device on the Internet) sees only your public IP – an IP associated with the device that has access to the Internet.

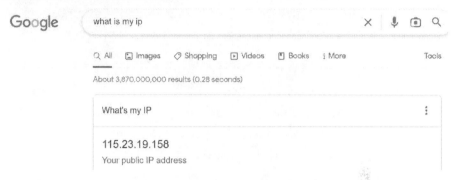

Figure 13. An example of a public IP

It may be a router on your Internet Service Provider side. That device hides all the specifics of your local network setup, so outside systems cannot directly access devices on your local network; it becomes the task for that device to reroute the **traffic** (flow of data) correctly to the proper device.

Sometimes, you can also add a **port** to that address. A port is a unique number assigned to identify a connection endpoint and to direct data to a specific service running on the receiving device. Within the network card, there will be multiple ports that receive data streams from the network. Different applications on the computer may use different ports for the exchange of data. When directing a data flow to a particular port, you tell the computer which application should be processing the data once it is received. For example, port "443" means we are sending encrypted web-traffic used by HTTPS protocol. Every time you open a website with the "https://" prefix, it means that the data flows between ports 443 in participating computers. A port is added after the address separated by a colon like this: **115.23.19.158:443**

All of this is not that dissimilar to how an old school post office works. Let's have a look.

Imagine you need to send a letter to your aunt or any other favourite relative. You write the postal code, the street address and then the name of the recipient. The postal code is similar to the network id in an IP address. It details which network to send the message to, just like a postal code details which region to send the letter to.

The address is similar to the host id which is used to find the destination within the network. Just like the street address gives the exact location of a house, the host id directs you to which device within the network the message should be sent to.

And finally, you've got your recipient's name. This is used to ensure the correct person receives the letter once it reaches the building. This is also what the port number does: it ensures the correct application processes the message within your host computer.

Alright, I hope it all makes sense. Networking is kind of confusing and we have barely scratched the surface. Feel free to google these topics and read more specialised sources if your job requires you to figure it out in more detail, because it's not an easy concept to explain in a few words. The next lesson, however, is going to be even more difficult to understand. We will talk about the protocols that help networks transmit data in a way that computers can understand them.

Lesson 14: Overview of OSI and TCP/IP

In this lesson we will talk about how networks operate and transmit data. It is a lot to comprehend, and some people devote their whole careers to learn this stuff. The good news is that most of it is automated and abstracted from end users, so unless you play a role in a networking infrastructure or security team, most of this will be hidden from you. It's still a good idea to know how it works at a high level though as questions of networking do arise in solution architecture and requirements conversations. As a delivery professional, you will use this knowledge to facilitate solution investigations and help unblock your team.

All the data transfer between the nodes in the network (different computers and other devices) is possible thanks to an OSI model. The OSI model is a conceptual model that explains the different levels of information exchange streams (also called abstraction levels).

The **OSI Model** (Open Systems Interconnection Model) is a conceptual framework used to describe the functions of a networking system. The OSI model characterises computing functions into a universal set of rules and requirements in order to support interoperability between different products and software.

It sees the network as a set of layers, each higher layer adds a level of extra meaning to the information transmitted via lower layers. All layers work together at the same time, focusing on enabling a different level of data exchange between the nodes in a network.

7	Application	Provide a user interface for sending and receiving data
6	Presentation	Encrypt, format, and compress data for transmission
5	Session	Initiate and terminate a session with the remote system
4	Transport	Break the data stream into smaller segments and provide reliable and unreliable data delivery
3	Network	Provide logical addressing
2	Data Link	Prepare data for transmission
1	Physical	Move data between devices

Figure 14. Layers of the OSI model

The table above summarises the layers. Each lower-level layer makes a higher-level layer possible, e.g., the existence of a physical layer (physical wires, etc.) allows for a data link layer to establish a connection between two nodes using those wires. When a data link is established, it allows for a network layer to use IPs for logical addressing, and so on. Let's zoom in on what every layer of this model does. We will start from the top and work our way down.

Application layer (layer 7):

At the very top of the OSI Reference Model, we find the Application layer which is implemented by the network applications. These are the applications that run on computers. The applications produce data to be transferred over the network. This layer also serves as a user interface that people can interact with when working with network apps. For example, when you interact with your internet browser, you are effectively interfacing with layer 7 of the OSI. This layer deals with complex protocols for information exchanges; some standards and protocols processed by applications include FTP for file transfer, SMTP for emails, and HTTP for web traffic.

FTP (File Transfer Protocol) is a network protocol for transmitting files between computers over network connections. It effectively allows the exchange of files between nodes.

SMTP (Simple Mail Transfer Protocol) is a protocol used in sending and receiving email. SMTP is used most commonly by email clients, including, but not limited to, Gmail, Outlook, Apple Mail and Yahoo Mail.

The Hypertext Transfer Protocol (HTTP) is the foundation of the World Wide Web and is used to load web pages using hypertext links.

All these protocols are application layer protocols designed to transfer information between networked devices, and they run on top of other layers of the network protocol stack.

Presentation layer (layer 6):

The presentation layer is also called the Translation layer. The data from the application layer is manipulated and reformatted here to be transmitted over the network.

Applications running on the local system may or may not understand the format that is used to transmit the data over the network. The presentation layer works as a translator. When receiving data from the Application layer, it converts that data into a format that can be sent over the network. When receiving data from the session layer, it reconverts the data into a format that the application, which will use it, can understand.

Session layer (layer 5):

This layer is responsible for the establishment of connection, maintenance of sessions, authentication, and security. It is responsible for setting up, managing, and dismantling sessions between presentation layer entities, and also for providing dialogs between computers.

When an application makes a network request, this layer checks whether the requested resource is available on a remote system, i.e. it tests if a network is available to make this connection.

Transport layer (layer 4):

Layer 4 is responsible for the end-to-end delivery of a complete atomic message. The transport layer also provides the acknowledgement of the successful data transmission and re-transmits the data if an error is found.

On the sending computer, it breaks the data stream into smaller pieces.

Each such piece is known as a **segment** and the process of breaking the data stream into smaller pieces is known as **segmentation**.

On the receiving computer, it joins all segments to recreate the original data stream.

This layer establishes a logical connection between the sending system and the receiving system and uses that connection to provide end-to-end data transportation. This process uses two protocols: TCP and UDP.

> **TCP** protocol is used for reliable data transportation. TCP is a connection-oriented protocol, which means the two systems first establish a connection which confirms both ends of data transmission are ready. Then it ensures the data sent by the sender is received by the receiver in full. It has built-in mechanisms for error detection and tries again if a failed transmission occurs, which adds to reliability but lengthens latency. It is a reliable but slower protocol.
>
> **UDP** protocol is used for time-sensitive data transportation. UDP is a connectionless protocol, it speeds up communications by not formally establishing a connection before data is transferred. It is less reliable, but much faster (up to 100x times faster).

Network layer (layer 3):

The network layer works for the transmission of data from one host to another across different networks. It also takes care of packet routing i.e., selection of the shortest path to transmit the packet, from the number of routes available.

This layer works with IP addresses and decodes them to route messages.

A **network packet** is a formatted unit of data. It consists of two parts: control information and user data; the latter is also known as the payload. Control information has data about the sender and the receiver of the packet and is used by network devices to send it accordingly. Payload stores meaningful user data that needs to be transmitted.

Packet routing or forwarding is the process of sending the packets from one network segment to another and selecting the optimal sequence of devices to get the data to where it needs to be.

Network layers are implemented by networking devices such as routers.

Data link layer (DLL) (layer 2):

The data link layer is responsible for the node-to-node delivery of the message. The main function of this layer is to make sure data transfer is error-free from one node to another, over the physical layer. While the physical layer sends electrical signals over wires, the data link ensures information is not lost and can be reconstructed from the signals.

When a packet arrives in a network, it is the responsibility of the DLL to transmit it to the Host using its MAC address.

Data link layer provides a way for a sender to transmit a set of bits that are meaningful to the receiver. This can be accomplished by attaching special bit patterns to the beginning and end of the meaningful piece of information, called a **frame**.

Physical layer (layer 1):

The lowest layer of the OSI reference model is the physical layer. It is responsible for the actual physical connection between devices. The physical layer contains information in the form of bits represented in electrical signals. It is responsible for transmitting individual bits from one node to the next. When receiving data, this layer will get the signal and convert it into 0s and 1s to send to the next layer.

Now, this is all abstract and technical. Let's use an example to see how it all works together. Imagine you are using a messenger app to send a message to your friend.

The messenger UI is **the application layer.** You use it to compose a message - write it down using natural language. You type it using your keyboard or on-screen keys and hit "Send".

The **presentation layer** encodes the data so that it can't be intercepted during the transmission, e.g., it applies encryption (we'll discuss how encryption works a bit later in the book).

The **session layer** creates a session between the two messengers – yours and your friend's. It checks that the friend is online and ready to accept the message. It is then converted into bits so it can be transmitted within the current session.

The **transport layer** breaks the data stream (the whole message) into smaller segments and delivers them one by one.

The **network layer** will attach the destination IP address and provide logical addressing through a series of routers, so each segment can be delivered to the right destination.

Finally, the **data link layer** will review hosts in the network to find which MAC address corresponds to the destination IP to send the data to it.

All of this will happen over a network of wires and radio waves and encoded into electric signals – that's **the physical layer**.

* * *

The OSI model has a few key characteristics. It introduces the separation of concerns between layers to provide reliable connection and data transmission. It's been around for about 40 years and... it is strictly speaking fictional.

I'm exaggerating a bit here. It is not like it does not exist, but it is a purely theoretical model that has never actually been truly built into production systems.

It is used as a theoretical basis for networking. OSI is implemented into production through more specialised protocols that implement elements of OSI.

For example, the internet is not based on the OSI model; it is based on a similar but simpler model called **TCP/IP**.

> **TCP/IP (Transmission Control Protocol/Internet Protocol)** is a suite of communication protocols used to interconnect network devices on the internet.
>
> TCP/IP is also used as a communications protocol in a private computer network (an intranet or extranet).

The Transfer Control Protocol/Internet Protocol (TCP/IP) is older than the OSI model and was created by the US Department of Defence. A key difference between the models is that TCP/IP is simpler, collapsing several OSI layers into one, see the table below.

OSI	TCP/IP
Application layer	Application layer
Presentation layer	
Session layer	
Transport layer	Transport layer
Network layer	Internet layer
Data link layer	Network access layer
Physical layer	

Figure 15. Comparison between OSI and TCP/IP layers

TCP/IP, unlike OSI, is a functional model. It is based on specific, standard protocols while OSI is a generic, protocol-independent model that was intended to describe all forms of network communication. So, how does TCP/IP work?

If we compare the two, we'll see that OSI layers 5, 6, and 7 are combined into one application layer in TCP/IP, so TCP/IP does not mandate layering of these functions.

OSI layers 1 and 2 are combined into one network access layer; so as long as someone (or rather something) takes care of physical transportations, TCP/IP does not specify how it is happening. It may happen on various physical transportation infrastructure implementations.

For each layer in the TCP/IP model there is a defined protocol that must be implemented by all systems participating in data exchange. Some layers allow for multiple protocols (e.g., TCP or UDP for the transport layer), so the system's developers may choose which one works better for their needs.

Lesson 15: World Wide Web: How websites work?

The internet is a network of networks that connects billions of digital devices worldwide. But how does it all work? When we type a website address in the browser to open a news outlet or an online store, we don't deal with MAC addresses or even IPs. Standard protocols allow for this to happen.

As we discussed above, your laptop or mobile phone will be connected to the web through a modem or router. Such devices are called **clients**.

When you type a URL in your browser, the browser sends the URL to the Internet Service Provider - a company that connects you to the internet and owns the infrastructure that supports it.

URL stands for **Uniform Resource Locator**. A URL is just a named address of a given unique resource on the Web. In theory, each valid URL points to a unique resource. A resource can be an HTML page, a styles document, an image, etc.

Any URL can be typed into your browser's address bar to tell it to load the associated page (resource).

A URL is composed of different parts, some mandatory and others optional.

Here is an example of how a URL is composed:

http://www.example.com:90/path/to/page.html?key=value#chapter

http:// - The scheme, or protocol, which tells your browser which protocol to use to retrieve the resource, e.g., http is a general web protocol, https is an encrypted secure protocol.

www.example.com:90 - This is called an authority and it consists of two parts: a domain and a port. The domain indicates the web server that you send a request to; think about it as "the website" that you address, e.g., google.com is an example of a domain. The port shows you which port on that server to send the request to (remember we discussed ports above? That's the same port here). A port can be omitted if you are using a standard port for your protocol (e.g., 80 for http or 443 for https).

/path/to/page.html – This is the path to the resource on the server. The files on the server are arranged similarly to how the files are located on your personal computer in a folder structure. This path shows which folders to go to and which file to pick from them.

?key=value - These are the extra parameters that you send to the server. These parameters are a list of key/value pairs separated with the & symbol. The Web server can use these parameters to perform certain actions before returning the resource. Each web server has its own list of parameters, which will often be pre-filled for you by another system, e.g., when you click an unsubscribe link from a newsletter, it will have something like "www.example.com/unsubscribe?email=youremail@gmail.com". This will tell the web page to use youremail@gmail.com as the address to unsubscribe from the newsletter.

#chapter - An anchor will scroll the page to a particular section when the browser opens it.

Inside the Internet Service Provider infrastructure, there are some servers called **Domain Name System servers** (DNS). DNS servers map URLs to IP addresses. This is how a human readable URL will convert into an IP address. This way you don't need to remember the IP addresses of the websites you use; you just type the human readable address and the DNS will translate it to an IP so that your browser can request a webpage from it.

When the browser gets a URL address, it sends a Hypertext Transfer Protocol (HTTP) request to the IP address returned by DNS and receives a response in the form of the confirmation of the request and the webpage contents (as a series of data packets) to show to the user. The browsers are responsible for interpreting the server answer and presenting it to the user in a graphical form.

The computer on the other side (the one that responds to requests) is called a **server** and it **hosts** the website.

In a nutshell, to have a website on the internet you need to write an application that generates web pages and sends them back via TCP/IP protocol based on the requests it receives from clients. This application requires a server to host it, and you need to register a domain name associated with the IP address of the server, so the DNS system is aware of it.

Once a webpage is received by the browser, the browser **renders** it, or interprets the HTML code to construct the static elements of the page. It can also execute parts of the page that contain executable commands (written in JavaScript code) in order to display the dynamic parts of the page. For example, you may have a website that shows the current score of a football game. The score message box can be static (because it does not change after the webpage is loaded) but the content of the box can update based on the current message broadcasted by the server. This will be asynchronously shown inside the box - and requires dynamic elements such as JavaScript scripts.

Some webpages are completely dynamic, meaning they are constructed algorithmically inside the browser; the server returns just the executable code (a series of commands) performed by the browser. Some webpages are completely static, meaning the server fully configures the webpage before sending it back to the client, and the browser just displays it as is without the need to follow any commands. Some webpages are a mixture of both.

Useful links for section 3

1. **Head First Networking**, by **Al Anderson, Ryan Benedetti**
   A quite unique book (like others in the Head First series) with visually rich content to ease your way into networking. A "light" reading on networks, if such a thing exists.

2. **Networking Essentials: A CompTIA Network+ N10-008 Textbook**, by **Jeffrey S. Beasley, Piyasat Nilkaew**
   CompTIA Network+ is an industry standard certification for network engineers. The preparation book (this one or any other) might be the best way to learn networks on quite a deep level. It is hard though, like really complex networking stuff.

3. **https://www.hp.com/us-en/shop/tech-takes/how-does-the-internet-work**
   A nice infographic by HP explaining how the internet works.

4. **https://developer.mozilla.org/en-US/docs/Learn/Common_questions/Web_mechanics**
   A great resource on how the internet works and the mechanics behind it by Mozilla, the company that created the Firefox browser. They have a lot of useful information for web developers on their website; feel free to explore.

< this page is intentionally left blank >

Section 4: Automation

< this page is intentionally left blank >

Lesson 16: What is automation?

Now we've come to the point in the course where we will see how IT can help in making standard operations of the business easier. We are talking about the concept of automation.

Automation is a term for technology applications that aim to minimise additional human activity to execute a task or business process.

> **Automation** is the creation and application of technologies to produce and deliver goods and services with minimal human intervention.

Basic automation takes simple, rudimentary tasks and automates them, so they are performed by an IT system and not a human operator. This level of automation is about digitising work by using tools to streamline and centralise routine tasks.

Imagine you release a new product, and you need to inform your marketing agencies to include information about it in their materials and to start advertising. It can be done by hand: a marketing coordinator may compile new material and send it out to each agency. But because the information shared with the agencies is identical, and the timing is as well, how good would it be to create one message for everyone and then let a piece of software send it to all of them at once? This is a simple example of automation.

Another example could be producing monthly activity reports based on data available in the IT system, e.g., a summary sent to the company's board including the total number of orders, profits and losses for the previous month. As long as the data is available, it doesn't have to be a human operator that calculates the totals and copies and pastes them into the slide deck – this process can be automated.

There are multiple types of automation, depending on which task is being automated. You may be involved in workflow or **business process automation** when repeatable business operations are executed by a piece of software; **decision making automation** when a piece of software helps select the best alternative; or **robotic process automation** focusing on eliminating routine cross systems tasks, etc.

Today, we can see the role that machine learning and AI are playing in automation more and more; we're starting to use the smarts in machines to automate complex elements of the business more regularly.

Let's have a closer look at some popular types of automation, starting with business processes.

Lesson 17: Business process automation

Business process automation (BPA), also known as business automation or, sometimes, digital transformation, is the technology-enabled automation of complex business processes.

Digital transformation is the process by which companies embed technologies across their operations to drive fundamental change. Business process automation plays a big role in it, and sometimes both terms are used interchangeably. However, often when people say digital transformation they mean huge changes to the way the organisation behaves, including changes to how it is structured, its values and fundamental beliefs. Business process automation when used as a term usually refers to automation of a single selected process, and not changing the whole enterprise.

The benefits of doing it are obvious. Making business simpler and more predictable, increasing service quality, or containing costs are just some examples. But how does one go about it?

At the core, business process automation is achieved by integrating multiple applications so they allow for a seamless flow of work according to a set of defined business logic. For this to work, you often need to not only build those applications and/or integrations between them, but also to change the organisational structure to support the new infrastructure, e.g., with new tools and technologies automating work, you need staff trained to operate, troubleshoot and fix those tools. However, the first step is to come up with a list of processes that need automation, and then define the boundaries of that automation, i.e., the scope of the project.

It is important to make sure we understand what we mean when we say "process"; otherwise, any automation might be challenging.

> According to some definitions, a **business process** is an end-to-end set of activities which collectively responds to an event, and transforms information, materials, and other resources into outputs that deliver value directly to the customers of the process. It may be internal to an organisation, or it may span several organisations.
>
> This definition is from A Guide to the Business Analysis Body of Knowledge® (BABOK® Guide). I have, however, found that there are many more definitions of a business process elsewhere, which indicates it is a bit of a hard concept to define. Anyway, let's stick with the definition above as a starting point.

In general, a business process:

1. **Involves work.** It can be described as a set of activities or as a sequence of steps and decisions. This work may

be performed by a human or a machine, or by a combination of both.

2. **Can be described in a "verb-noun" form.** It is not a super formal definition, yet can be used as a simple and effective step to scope out a process. If you can name some activity this way, it is likely a business process. If you can't it is likely something else. Let's have a look at a few examples. "Acquire new customer" is a good candidate to be a process. You've got an object that is transformed via some activity, so it may as well be a business process. "Customer relationship management" is probably not a good example. It does not concern a specific object, thus does not have a specific result, and is likely a collection of processes. Which brings us to the next point...

3. **Delivers a specific essential result.** The result of a process must be discrete and identifiable, in a sense that you can differentiate individual instances of the result. In our example above, "Acquire a customer" implies having an individual customer acquired is a result. The result is also measurable. You can how many of those results were produced in a given time or by a single instance of a process. And the result should be essential. It is a fundamentally necessary outcome for the business, not just a consequence or by-product of some activities.

4. **Initiated by a specific trigger**. A trigger can be an action, a temporal event, a condition or a rule; but any process must have a defined starting point.

Once the process candidate for automation is defined, it is usually modelled using a formal notation so that it can be analysed. This is called an as-is analysis of a business process.

As-is process analysis or **current state analysis** is an activity that identifies and evaluates current processes of the business. Current state analysis can focus on an entire business organisation or on one or more specific processes within a department or team.

The result of as-is analysis will be a set of documented findings from evaluating the current processes. The goal is to formalise the current state of play - how the organisation operates today - and to identify any inefficiencies or pain points of the current process. Resolving these pain points will be a task for automation.

You rarely want to automate the current state as-is, because the current processes will not be optimised for automation. They have evolved in a world without the solution that you are putting forward, so some steps can become inefficient or redundant in the future. Plus, if you are disrupting the current processes anyway, why not use the opportunity and make them a bit better.

Once you've done your analysis you end up with a list of potential improvements to the process. Now you need to identify which improvements to address via automation. Some problems are good candidates for automation (e.g., repetitive decision making, algorithmic updates, etc.) and some are not, these include things such as ad hoc decisions, elements of the process requiring moral judgement or a personal touch, etc. Prioritise your improvements and move on to the next step.

Once you know the current state and the list of issues you need to solve, it is time to design a future state (or to-be state). This will be a blueprint for how the process will work with the help of a new automation solution.

While the as-is analysis maps where your processes are, the to-be analysis (**future state analysis**) maps where you want them to be. The as-is phase outlines the current state of your processes and any gaps or issues with your current mode of operation. The to-be process mapping documents how you want your processes to be.

Often when documenting a process, you will use a **formal process modelling notation**. A process modelling notation is a graphical representation for specifying business processes in a business process model. A notation will tell you which visual objects to use and what they mean in the context of a business process. It will also dictate how different objects can relate to each other and where they can be positioned in the model.

Following a defined notation helps you align on the understanding of the models, so multiple people can work on the same model and the results will be compatible with each other and understood by all participants.

There are a few common notations, such as BPMN (Business Process Model and Notation), eEPC (Extended Event-driven Process Chain), UML (Unified Modelling Language) Activity Diagram, UPN (Universal Process Notation), etc.

When you've got the results of both your as-is and to-be analysis, you can compare the two and understand the gaps - the differences between the two states. These differences need to be addressed in your automation project.

Once the opportunities for automation are identified, the company will decide on the way forward. The options include automating using existing software; the purchasing, or developing, of new products; or using an off-the-shelf process automation suite.

Process automation suites allow you to convert the model of a business process into an executable flow, without coding.

Imagine, you've got a simple business process: an employee requests a day off, a manager approves or rejects it, and then an HR officer gets notified about it. In the days of old this would be done verbally or via email.

Today, with the help of a process automation engine, someone can create a process model using formal notation and associate each process step with a form that asks for a defined set of fields to be filled in. When complete, they can press a button to convert the model into software. Once converted, the employee will have access to another form that is sent to a person tagged as their manager in the system; and once that person approves the request a notification is sent to an HR system.

Such approaches are often called **low-code** or **no-code** automation. Low-code automation refers to software that lets business teams build and automate their processes and workflows without coding skills or experience. Instead, they use a visual interface to make changes and access features.

Of course, in the case of a standard business process like that you don't need to create your own product or even use process automation suites. Most likely, there is a third-party solution that comes with this type of automation. For example, the management of leave requests is a fairly typical part of any HR system.

When deciding which approach to automation to use, consider the following:

1. Is it a standard process that is likely to be automated in a third-party solution?
2. Is it a process that can be automated with no-code or low-code solutions?
3. Or is the process complex and unique enough to warrant bespoke development?

The example above is a simple 3-step process to help you select what type of process automation you need. We are just moving an offline workflow into digital so that it has a digital footprint. But even a simple process like this can be further improved through automation. The next lesson will show us how.

Lesson 18: Decision automation

It might surprise you, but one of the most crucial metrics for any business is the speed at which they make decisions.

A business faces hundreds if not thousands of decisions a day. It has been estimated that a project budgeted at $1 million in labour costs will encounter about 1000 decisions; and one budgeted at $10 million will generate about 10,000 decision points (this is according to a report by the Standish Group, *CHAOS 2020: Beyond Infinity*).

If each decision takes at least an hour of someone's time, and that someone is billed to the project at a rate of $200/hour, the decisions alone will cost $2 million on a $10 million project, or no less than 20% of the total budget!

So, the more you can simplify and automate decision making, the more money you can save for the organisation through an investment in IT. That is, by the way, a very common metric when it comes to measuring the success of automation: how much time it saves.

Imagine a simple example from the previous lesson – a person going on leave. When considering whether to approve the leave request or not, the manager needs to consider if the workload allows for it, but also if the person is eligible for leave. There may be a policy in the company that explains how many days of leave a person can apply for and what the rules are if the person takes extra leave, e.g. whether a person can take credit for leave.

For the sake of this example, let's say in the policy: a person is eligible for 20 days of annual leave, and they can go as much as 5 days into a negative leave balance if they have passed their probation and are not serving their notice period. In addition to this, the negative balance cannot be applied to taking leave directly before or after a public holiday.

This is quite a rule, right? However, as a rule it is deterministic and repeatable. It means that giving a situation the result of the decision making is always the same, which means it can be automated.

IT teams use **decision models** to first standardise the decision logic, and then implement it in automation engines. There are generally two main approaches to modelling decisions: 1) via decision trees and 2) via decision tables. In general, any decision tree can be represented as a decision table - it is a matter of aesthetics and readability of the model. Simpler models with less parameters are often easier modelled using trees, complex models with more decision parameters are often easier modelled via a table.

Let's have a look at our simple process from the previous lesson:

Apply for leave -> Approve the leave request -> Inform an HR officer

There is an implicit decision step there to approve the leave request. It may go either way: the request may be approved, but it may be rejected. Often it is an automated decision based on the person's situation, and such a decision can be modelled using a decision tree.

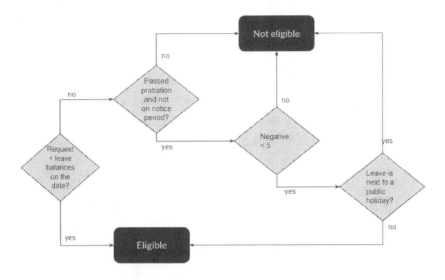

Figure 16. An example of a decision tree for an eligibility check

Here is how to read it: go from left to right, each diamond is a decision point. Based on the decision, you take one or the other path forward. The first diamond checks the state of the leave balance. If the requested number of days is less than the amount of leave days the person has accumulated, it allows the person to take the leave. If the amount is more than the accumulated one, it becomes trickier, and the decision logic checks for other conditions.

If, according to the decision logic in the system, the person is eligible to take leave, we can proceed to the human approval by the manager (based on workload). Otherwise, we automatically reject the request, saving everybody a bunch of time and avoiding any potential policy violation.

Using a formal model like this helps with clarifying the logic.

A decision table is very similar to a decision tree, but it presents the information in a different format. Here is an example of it.

Leave balance after the leave	Passed probation?	Notice period?	More than 5 in negative?	Next to a public holiday?	Verdict
positive	n/a	n/a	n/a	n/a	eligible
negative	no	n/a	n/a	n/a	not eligible
negative	yes	yes	n/a	n/a	not eligible
negative	yes	no	yes	n/a	not eligible
negative	yes	no	no	yes	not eligible
negative	yes	no	no	no	eligible

Figure 17. A decision table

Every column except for the last one represents an input parameter to the model. The last column represents a verdict of the decision. In our case, we've got 5 questions. Depending on the answers to those questions, the verdict will be different.

When decisions are modelled using these formal notations, it helps to convert a decision-making process into an algorithm which can be automated.

Lesson 19: Robotic process automation

Robotic process automation or RPA is a very trendy topic today; let's discuss it.

An RPA consists of three elements:

1. **Robotic:** There is a robot at the core of the automation. We define a "robot" as an entity that has the capability to mimic human actions, to pretend it is a human carrying out the work.

2. **Process**: RPA is concerned with automating sequences of steps that lead to a meaningful result - a business process.

3. **Automation**: When RPA happens, it happens with minimal human intervention, or with none at all.

So basically, when we are talking about RPA, we mean automating business processes in a way that would very closely mimic a human performing them, just without the human.

I came across this quote some time ago, "the goal of RPA is to take a robot out of a human, and to let humans focus on human tasks while the robot does the tedious repetitive steps".

Let's zoom in on how this works.

At the core of RPA is a special piece of software that can mimic human actions within an operating system.

An **operating system** (OS) is system software that manages computer hardware and software resources and provides common services for applications. The OS serves as an interim agent between software applications and hardware parts, ensuring enough hardware resources are allocated for the applications to run.

Operating systems are found on many devices that represent a computer: mobile phones, ATMs, video game consoles, personal computers, etc. Microsoft Windows, MacOS and Linux are some of the most popular operating systems.

Let's say you have a website that needs to be updated based on a new brand and marketing content brief. A copywriter has prepared a lot of new text for the website and now it needs to be updated on all pages. Tasks like opening a file, copying its content, opening a website, pasting the content, and submitting a form to save it take a lot of time for content entry personnel (the people who update content on the website).

This is an amazing task for RPA. Robot software can do it all as well (open files, copy content, paste it inside another program and click a button). However, being a robot, it does it faster and with less human errors (e.g. copy-pasting the wrong piece of content on the wrong page).

RPA takes a different approach to more standard process automation. Instead of natively integrating software components with the use of APIs like we described before, it takes human enabled workarounds and automates those. It effectively hijacks your operating system and performs actions as if a human performed them, mimicking human input so it is interpreted by the operating system the same way.

This approach works well with legacy systems which are hard to integrate with, or with software packages developed by third parties where you don't have the means to change them to fit your processes. So instead of finding ways to connect to these applications via APIs, you could implement an RPA robot that will manipulate the operating system making those applications believe they have received input from a human actor.

In our previous process example (an annual leave request), imagine that an HR person needs to run a regular report on people taking leave and then prepare a slide for a PowerPoint presentation with this data. This forms a part of the executive deck presented every month. Of course, a human can open the HR system, get a report of all of the people taking leave this month, count them and update the slides but... this feels like a kind of boring and robotic action. So, it is a great candidate for robotic automation. Instead of doing it all every time, an HR person may trigger an RPA bot which will log into the HR system to run the report, calculate the number of people, and update a particular line in the PowerPoint presentation on behalf of a human. And it will do it much faster than the human would do it because it does not hesitate or get distracted.

To create an RPA bot, often a company will use special software that is designed for this task. Often such software will come with a toolkit for bot creation, for example a tool that will record the actions to repeat them in the future. Such tools speed up bot creation. Instead of programming all the steps, you just need to review how they are recorded and adjust the input as needed. For example, where you interact with a particular file or line within a file, you may want to make the rule more general, so the bot picks up the next file on every run, or the next line. This way it won't override results of the previous step but will keep adding information. A few minor tweaks like this, and your bot is ready.

So, bot creation may be as simple as:

1. Turn on the recorder
2. Perform the steps once
3. Review how the steps are recorded and fine tune the actions
4. Run the bot when you need it

Of course, some processes are more complex than this and will require more in-depth programming to accommodate for business logic or to perform complex actions, so RPA is not only a record-and-play exercise – but it is an option to get started.

Lesson 20: Machine learning and AI

Historically, humans and machines used to be good at different things. As we discussed above, highly repetitive tasks that require a lot of attention to detail are the primary candidates for automation, while tasks requiring a level of cognition or creativity were predominantly left for humans.

However, this did not stop the research on computer applications that can perform such human tasks. This branch of research is commonly referred to as Artificial intelligence (AI).

Artificial Intelligence (AI) is a branch of computer science that aims to create intelligent machines - machines that can perform tasks which typically require human intelligence. AI is based on the idea of building computer systems that can simulate human thought processes, such as learning, reasoning, perception, and decision-making.

Generally speaking, AI technology can be divided into two main categories:

1. **Narrow** (or weak) AI: Systems that are designed to perform specific tasks, such as image recognition or natural language processing. You can think about these as tools to perform a single specialised task, but with the use of AI technology.

2. **General** (or strong) AI: Systems that can perform any intellectual task that a human can; think about these as a smart assistant who can pick up any task.

When speaking about AI, people often discuss the application of machine learning. Machine learning (ML) is a type of artificial intelligence (AI) that allows computer systems to learn and improve from experience without being explicitly programmed. Just like humans are born to the world knowing a little and over time learning from the patterns they observe, ML solutions are built without pre-recorded knowledge. ML is based on the idea that machines can learn from data, identify patterns, make predictions, and adjust their behaviour accordingly.

In the technology world, machine learning is widely used in situations where unobvious patterns in data need to be identified and used to make predictions or explain observed phenomena.

One of the key advantages of machine learning is its ability to automate complex tasks and make predictions with a high degree of accuracy. This makes it an invaluable tool for businesses and organisations looking to streamline operations, increase efficiency, and make data-driven decisions. Here are some examples of solutions using ML:

1. Predictive analytics: Machine learning can be used to analyse historical data and make predictions about the future, such as customer behaviour or market trends. This can help businesses make more informed decisions about product development, marketing strategies, and sales forecasting.
2. Fraud detection: Machine learning algorithms can be trained to detect fraudulent activity, such as credit card or insurance fraud. This can help businesses identify and prevent fraudulent transactions before they occur,

saving them money and reducing the risk of reputational damage.

3. Personalization: Machine learning can be used to personalise customer experiences by analysing data about their behaviour and preferences. This can help businesses tailor their marketing messages, recommend products, and improve customer satisfaction.

4. Supply chain optimization: Machine learning can be used to optimise supply chain operations, such as inventory management and logistics.

5. Chatbots: Machine learning can be used to develop chatbots that can handle customer inquiries and support requests. This can help businesses provide 24/7 customer support and reduce the workload on human customer service agents.

These are just some examples which I hope help you understand the possibilities and scope of ML and AI applications.

Lastly, we need to discuss what Generative AI is.

Generative AI, also known as creative AI, is a type of artificial intelligence that is capable of creating new and original content, such as images, videos, or music, based on a set of input parameters. Just like other ML models, it learns the common patterns from an enormous amount of data; but in addition to remembering these patterns it also has mechanisms to reproduce them based on a request. This is probably one of the newest branches of AI, which has caused a noticeable hype in the industry with tools such as ChatGPT (text generation), Midjourney and DALL·E (image generation), etc.

Such tools can prove to be a lot of help in areas like content creation (production of videos or images, blog posts, marketing campaigns, etc.), product design, simulation (generation of multiple possible scenarios based on the same input to ensure the product or process that you build will accommodate for those), and innovation (coming up with new ideas and solutions).

The role of generative AI in business is still emerging and is yet to be refined considering the obvious benefits of such tools but also concerns of security and ethics. Don't get fooled by the industry hype: these tools cannot generate new knowledge (or any knowledge), they can just compose digital bits (be it words, or sounds, or images) to follow the patterns the ML model has seen in the real world. So, there is no proof the data the ML model is trained on is relevant (or true at all) or is sourced from legitimate sources, nor is there any way to check if the result of such generation is consistent or usable or truthful.

In the spirit of practising what you preach I did try to write this lesson with the use of generative AI. It helped to formulate some initial ideas and layout of the lesson, but required such heavy editing that I'm not actually sure how much time I saved overall. I could have just cited a few more traditional sources and written the rest from scratch :)

Useful links for section 4

1. **Practical Process Automation**, by **Bernd Ruecker**
   This book demonstrates how to leverage process automation technology such as workflow engines to orchestrate software, humans, decisions, or bots. It is full of examples and use cases and is a good book for anyone interested in learning automation (especially in a developer or architect role). However, it is quite technical and requires knowledge of programming to get through the examples.

2. **Automate the Boring Stuff with Python**, by **Al Sweigart**
   A nice book full of cookbook type recipes to automate simple admin tasks using the Python programming language. It is quite technical, but is easy to follow and lets you get your hands on simple automation.

3. **Workflow Modeling: Tools for Process Improvement and Application Development**, by **Alec Sharp**, **Patrick McDermott**
   This is my favourite book on process modelling and running process optimisation and automation. An absolute must read if you work in the process automation field; and, unlike the books above, it is designed more for analysts and managers than software developers.

4. **https://powerautomate.microsoft.com/en-us/what-is-rpa/**
   Power Automate is an RPA solution from Microsoft. This article gives a very quick and opinionated overview of what RPA is; but feel free to click around and learn more about the platform on the website or pick a book explaining how to use it and build your own bots. Power

Automate is not the only RPA solution but it is very popular because it is a part of the Microsoft suite of products for business and it integrates natively with other Microsoft products.

5. **https://openai.com/blog/chatgpt**
   ChatGPT, a generative AI product by openai, is probably the most spoken about AI tool in 2023. Have a look at what it is if you have not yet.

< this page intentionally left blank >

Section 5: Data management

Data storage

Databases

Distributed data storages and cloud computing

Data analysis

< this page is intentionally left blank >

Lesson 21: Data storage

When we talk about information systems or information technology, we often consider not only the applications or hardware parts, but also the data that the application processes. Depending on the type of system, it may source, manipulate, and store different types of data.

For this to happen, we need to provide applications with data storage where the data will rest waiting to be picked up by our software. So how does this work?

Using a piece of paper and pen, you can store data on that piece of paper by scribbling notes, letters, or drawings on it. Computer storage works in a similar manner. Inside the computer there is a unit that changes its state to store data. Unlike a pen and paper solution it has an ability to rewrite the information stored on it (in most cases), so the memory storage can be reused. Similar to using a pencil: you need to erase the old information to reuse your storage.

How does it work? On the lowest level of computing, any information is represented as a series of 0s and 1s. Anything more complex is getting encoded into 0s and 1s.

The way computers represent information as strings of 0s and 1s is called **binary code**. Any sequence of ones and zeros is binary code, with each of those sequences being a unique set of instructions.

There are many ways of representing data as binary code (called **encoding**). In the early days of computing, most computers used 8-bit code, which could represent only 4 billion different strings of ones and zeros. Modern computers use much larger code, allowing for over a trillion different strings. How these code strings are represented depends on the computer, the code format, and the software.

But why do we only use 0s and 1s? Electrical currents are either running (open/on) or they're not (closed/off) meaning that inside an electrical circuit we have two value characters available to us: on and off, or 1 and 0 respectively. This is a fundamental constraint on any computing system - to store or operate on data it needs to be represented as a series of 0s and 1s, otherwise there is no means of encoding the data in a way meaningful to a computer.

Inside a computer there is a storage device that has a magnetic tape in it. The device takes the information encoded in a way that a computer understands (as a series of binary code, 0s and 1s) and writes them as magnetic north or south onto tiny sections of that device. When the data needs to be retrieved, the same device goes through those areas and reads whether there is a magnetic north or south, converting those to 0s and 1s and sending them as a digital signal back to the central processing unit to interpret the signal. This is how a hard drive works.

A hard drive or **hard disk drive (HDD)** is a type of data storage device. It looks like what you see below. There is a part that looks like a platter where the magnetic film is (the film is very tiny, you can't really see it), there is the reading head that reads and writes data, and there is a separate device called an actuator that moves it (this consists of a moving arm that holds the reading head and a static part that has all the controls for the disk).

Figure 18. HDD
Image source: https://en.wikipedia.org/wiki/Hard_disk_drive#/media/File:Laptop-hard-drive-exposed.jpg CC BY-SA 3.0

An HDD is what is called a "non-volatile" storage drive, which means it can retain the stored data even when no power is supplied to the device. Its main drawback is that to read or write information from the magnetic tape the head needs to go around the drive and physically read each section. It is a comparatively slow process.

This process can be improved with the use of **SSD** (solid state disks). Whereas hard disk drives use a spinning magnetic disk and a mechanical write head to manipulate data, SSDs use electronic circuits to store and retrieve data. We are getting technical here, but the main point is that SSDs are faster than HDDs and consume less energy (as they don't have moving parts). The main drawback is that due to the nature of the technology used, the SSD's lifespan is generally shorter. Anyway, both types of disks can be used to store data long term and retrieve it quickly enough that it can be consumed by computer applications. However, both types of drives are not fast enough for the real time data processing required by the CPU (central processing unit) to actively perform calculations, as they both take time to perform the read-write action.

CPUs (**central processing units**) can be found in almost all electronic devices (computers, mobile phones, smart watches, smart TVs, etc.). A CPU processes and executes instructions and acts as the brain of a device. A CPU consists of billions of microscopic transistors placed onto a single computer chip used to perform the calculations needed to run programs. They are effectively switches that turn on or off to represent the ones or zeros which encode all the information processed by the device. Any command executed by a computer goes through the CPU. In order for this to happen quickly, the data used in the calculations needs to be readily accessible for the CPU; and the HDDs and SSDs tend to be too slow for this.

This is when we introduce **RAM (rapid access memory)**. It is the fastest memory available at the fingertips of the CPU and is used for data that is actively being manipulated right now. RAM is used to store the computer programs and data that the CPU needs in real time. RAM is made up of semiconductors and it maintains its current state only when it is powered on; if you remove the power the data will be lost. This makes RAM a "volatile" data storage.

That is exactly what happens when you turn off your computer. It "forgets" which programs are open, so when you turn it back on it boots up in a blank state. This is because your RAM gets flushed when you power off. However, if you put your computer into a hibernation state, it stores a copy of the current RAM onto your HDD or SSD, so it can be retrieved upon waking up. This way you still retain the active state even if the computer is powered off; however, it takes the computer a while to read the data from the non-volatile storage and load it back to RAM - this is what happens during the computer boot time.

When you are developing IT systems, there are two important data-related factors:

1. How much data should be stored in "non-volatile" (permanent) memory storage
2. How much data needs to be loaded into RAM for processing at any given moment in time

These two factors will dictate the data storage requirements needed for your program to perform.

However, when it comes to permanent memory, it is not only the question of how much and what data you will need to store, it is also a question of a specific method of doing so. For example, you can always decide to store your data on your local computer. However, this is not always possible and you need to design a more complex distributed memory solution where data storage is available via networks. In this case, the computer executing the logic will request the data via a networking interface. Another thing to consider is what format the data is stored in so that it can be consumed and properly interpreted by the application (we spoke about this briefly when discussing APIs - a similar concept is applied here, data needs to be stored in a format that your application can read and work with).

So now we are talking not just about storing raw data on memory devices but also about structuring the data for reuse. Databases play a big role in this process, and we are going to discuss them in the next lesson.

Lesson 22: Databases

Imagine you need to store some information about your customers on a computer, so that you can retrieve it later. For example, you want to use this information in your marketing communications. How would you go about this task?

Of course you can just dump all the data into a single text file, but you will need a human to read and interpret this data. For data to become machine readable and usable, it needs to have metadata: data about data, stored in a pre-defined format.

> Examples of metadata could be special labels that explain which value in your data corresponds to the customer's name, address, etc.
>
> **Metadata** (or **metainformation**) is "data that provides information about other data" but not the content of the data, such as the text of a message or the image itself. In the context of data management and manipulation, you need some pointers on how to find the right data for your operation. For example, if you want to address your customer via their first name in an email, you need to know which data element contains the first name; thus, you need some metadata explaining how the content of the data is structured.

Imagine a spreadsheet; you have columns for different types of data, and rows for individual records.

	A	B	C	D	E	F
1	name	surname	email	phone		
2						
3						
4						
5						
6						
7						
8						
9						
10						
11						
12						

Figure 19. A very simple spreadsheet structure for your data

For example, you may have a name, a surname, an email, a phone number and so on. All of these are columns and when filled with content across a row they describe the same customer. In this case, the column labels will serve as metadata, they describe what the data in the columns is about.

In this format, data becomes machine accessible. You can instruct a computer to find a customer with the name of "John Constantine" and retrieve their email address. Or ask it to retrieve every phone number of every customer so you can send a mass text campaign. Or have it find the email of a customer who has just called you (using their phone number) to follow up on their request via an email. And so on.

This is how metadata plus structure helps make data usable. And this brings us to the concept of a database.

A **database** is an organised collection of structured information, or data, stored in a computer system. A database is managed by a special type of software called a **database management system** (DBMS). Together, the data and the DBMS are referred to as a database system, often shortened to just a database.

Data within the most common types of databases in operation today is typically modelled in rows and columns just like a spreadsheet. But instead of being stored in one sheet, it will be organised in a series of tables to make processing and data querying efficient.

Another difference between a spreadsheet and a database is the internal organisation of data within the system. Databases are designed for speed of use and scalability while spreadsheets are primarily designed for a single user; adding an ability to easily exchange files between users. Databases are designed to hold much larger collections of organised information, sometimes massive amounts of data. Databases allow multiple users to quickly and securely access and query the data using highly complex logic and language.

Otherwise, it is easy to think about databases as collections of tables similar to a spreadsheet. The different tables will have unique identifications (called IDs) for each record so that different records can link together.

Imagine, you have a table for Users which stores information about your customers. Then, you can create another table called Orders which will store information about the orders made by your users. For each order there is a user who places it. You could add all the details of the user to each order record, but... it wouldn't be ideal as this would create a lot of duplicate information in the system, and if you need to make changes to the user's name or address you will need to update every record of every order. What you would do instead is use a database to link the records.

You can have the details of an order in an Order record. Then instead of storing all the information about the user in the same records, you can just add a unique customer ID to it. This ID will be a link to a record of a unique customer who placed this order.

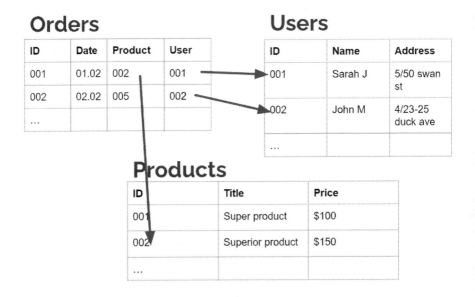

Figure 20. A simple representation of records linking to each other using unique IDs in a database.

When data is organised like this, we call it a **relational database**. There are some rules that database developers usually follow when designing the data structures to store the data. The most common one is data normalisation. The idea of normalisation is to do exactly what we did above - separate data points to reduce duplication and associate any meaningful information with a unique ID for ease of linking and search. There are other normalisation considerations of course (and different levels of normalisation) but we won't be covering them here.

Relational databases are not the only ones out there. The first databases were created early in the 1960s and they were not relational. - they were **navigational**. Navigational databases assume data has a hierarchy; they model data in a tree-like fashion, where parent data elements will have one or multiple child elements. This allows for **one-to-many** relationships (one parent may have multiple child elements, but a child element may have one and only one parent). So, you can't easily handle situations when one order may contain multiple product types, and at the same time one product type may appear in multiple orders. This is called a **many-to-many** relationship.

Network databases were introduced later as a more flexible model that allowed multiple relationships. Although network databases were more flexible in terms of database design, the implementation made them quite inflexible after the data had been loaded into a database.

In the 1980s, **relational databases** became popular. Even though they have been around for a while, relational databases are still in wide use today (with relational DBMSs still being the most popular database products today).

In the 1990s, following the popularity of object-oriented programming, **object-oriented databases** emerged. Instead of storing data as tables, they started to store it as objects. It gets a little technical here, but the key point is that object-oriented databases could store more complex data structures which allowed for a better ability to integrate with complex solutions. However, they received a lot of criticism for being slower in terms of performance and did not replace the relational databases.

More recently, as a response to the need for faster speed and the processing of unstructured data, new generations of databases were introduced, commonly referred to as **NoSQL**. These were not designed to replace relational databases, but to offer alternatives in scenarios where a traditional relational database would not perform well. For example, relational databases are notorious for not scaling horizontally well (this means you can't easily add more computers to share the workload on one database), so for huge amounts of data that requires such scaling a NoSQL approach may work better.

When your data sits in a relational database, you can manipulate it using special commands called SQL (**structured query language**).

SQL consists of specific commands and keywords that allow it to retrieve the data based on search parameters, manipulate data itself (e.g., add a new record or update a record), or change the structure of the database (create a new table, create a new column, or delete a table).

Here is an example of a simple command using SQL.

```
SELECT title, author
 FROM   Books
 WHERE  price > 100.00
 ORDER  BY title;
```

This will select all the titles and their authors from the table called "Books" where the price is larger than 100 units. Before presenting it to the user it will also order the resulting data by title in alphabetical order. And the best part: you can read this statement in (almost) plain English, and it makes sense. How cool is that?

That's the power of SQL. It is designed in a way that you compose it explicitly stating what you want it to do, and that's exactly how it is going to be interpreted by the system. The CAPITALISED words in the example are the key words. They have special meaning for the system and are executed as commands; the rest of the statement includes the parameters you can define to shape the query.

Here is a more complex example. This one may take a while to figure out and may require some understanding of how SQL works.

```
SELECT Books.title AS Title,
       count(*) AS Authors
 FROM   Books
 JOIN   Book_author
   ON   Books.isbn = Book_author.isbn
 GROUP  BY Books.title;
```

It still reads almost like plain English, but it does have a lot more going on. What we do here is select book titles and count the number of authors that a book has. For this to happen we **JOIN** two tables: "Books" to fetch the title and a new table "Book_author" to fetch all of the authors who have the current book listed as their book. This is done using a unique ID that all the books in the world have: an ISBN (International Standard Book Number). To join two tables, we need to have a piece of data that can tell you that two records are related. We use the **ON** keyword to do this. The statement after **ON** tells you that if the ISBN for a Book record matches the ISBN for a Book author record, then both records can be joined together as if they were coming from the same table.

SQL knowledge is often a requirement even for less technical jobs, such as analysts, solution operators, marketing specialists, etc. - anyone who has a need to retrieve data from databases.

But how does a database get connected with a software solution?

A database will be managed by a database management system (DBMS). It encapsulates a lot of admin tasks for managing data, including organising it on hard drives, indexing it for search, and running health checks. Typically, when you are creating a new software product, this product will connect to a database management solution via an API and is able to write, manipulate, and retrieve the data via that API, while leveraging the out of the box capabilities of a DBMS. Often, the software solution will compose SQL statements based on user input and pass them on to DBMS for execution. DBMS will then process the queries and send back the results of processing for the application to interpret and present to the user.

Lesson 24: Distributed storage and cloud computing

So far, we've been talking about local data storage. However, storing data locally all the time can be risky and difficult.

The more data you have, and the more critical that data is, the more control procedures will need to be applied to ensure that: it is not lost; it is secure; and it is readily accessible for the legitimate applications that need to use it. To achieve this companies and individuals often centralise their storage facilities.

They can do this within their own network using a network storage device (NAS, network attached storage). It is a special piece of hardware accessible via the local network by the computers from within that network. It is designed to serve as a location where the data is saved and can be accessed. Think about it as a shared disk that can be accessed from any computer in the network (providing access has been granted).

NAS is not the only network storage solution. Some other solutions that you may come across include:

- **SAN** (storage area network): A dedicated high-speed network that interconnects multiple servers with a range of storage devices. It is generally more flexible for users as it can process not only individual file requests but also manage related blocks of data. It is generally harder to set up compared to a NAS solution.

- **DAS** (direct-attached storage): Storage directly attached to a server device, e.g. an external hard drive connected via a cable. Other devices in the network cannot access the data directly; they will have to send requests to do so via the server that connects the DAS.

However, even network solutions like these can come with an overhead of managing a dearth of storage devices and related infrastructure. The main challenges of doing this include managing the availability of data, ensuring the data is not lost if there are infrastructure or software issues, securing the data, and implementing high performance requirements - so solutions using the data are not slowed down by underperforming data storage. When your hardware and software are both managed by your business in full, it's up to you and your team to manage, update, and replace each component of the infrastructure as needed. This requires a lot of specialist skill and accountability.

Losing your data is a big issue for any business. When an organisation manages its own solution for data storage, they need to pay close attention to ensure the data is not lost in an incident or catastrophic event. Any data storage device may break, sometimes unexpectedly. As we discussed above, disk drives are very complex devices that may malfunction or break due to wear and tear. Regular **data backups** are a must for a modern business. A backup, or data backup, is a copy of computer data taken and stored elsewhere so that it may be used to restore the original after a data loss event.

Another solution is to use data technology that can withstand the failure of a hard drive. This is called redundancy - duplicating elements of data in a way that allows reconstructing the full data set if part of it is missing. There are multiple ways of doing it, commonly known as **RAID** ("redundant array of inexpensive disks" or "redundant array of independent disks"). RAID is a technology that combines multiple physical disk drives into one or more logical drives for the purposes of data redundancy, performance improvement, or both. So an operating system will think it interacts with one drive, when in reality the data is physically stored on multiple drives. It is stored in a way that even if one drive fails, the operating system will be able to get the full data as if nothing failed (regardless of which drive from the array failed).

Combining data backups with technology for preventing loss helps mitigate some data related risks.

Some companies decide to do it themselves and invest in the infrastructure and support personnel because they see value in it. For instance, they deal with very sensitive data that requires special handling, or they are legally obliged to keep data within a particular country or jurisdiction.

This is called an **on-premises** IT infrastructure (IT infrastructure that your organisation owns and manages themselves). It presents the biggest level of responsibility to the company but gives you the most control.

For most commercial organisations it is not important where exactly their data is stored as long as it is secure and available. It is very popular to outsource your data needs to a specialised company (often one that owns a datacentre facility) who can perform all the maintenance and fine tuning for you, for a moderate fee.

A **datacentre** is a huge collection of hardware designed to host massive amounts of data and maintain massive CPU power. Think about it as a huge hanger type building stuffed with thousands of computers or complex technology to keep them all running and connected to the network.

As a client of such a datacentre, you will get access to a portion of the storage space and computing power available. For example, you may be a client of Amazon or Google. You purchase a subscription from them that gives you 5Tb of data and a certain amount of CPU processing time. You can use this to store your data and host your applications. This way you don't need to worry about having any servers of your own. The infrastructure is fully owned by the provider, and you receive a service from that provider in the form of dedicated space and power, with clearly defined service conditions (called SLAs - service level agreements). The more you are willing to pay, the more scaled the service becomes; that is, the more power, faster processing, and mode space you'll receive.

This is exactly how cloud computing works. The whole idea of a cloud is that it is light for the business - like a cloud. ;) You don't own the infrastructure, you borrow it and scale it as much as you need, and when you need it.

Cloud computing is often referred to as an "as-a-service" solution. There are three main types of these solutions, and they differ in the amount of service you get and in the amount of control you have.

Infrastructure-as-a-service, or **IaaS**, is one step away from having an on-premises infrastructure. It's a pay-as-you-go service where a third party provides you with infrastructure services, such as storage and virtualization, as you need them, via a cloud, through the Internet. Your organisation is still responsible for installing the operating systems and managing any data or applications, but a service provider gives you access to, and management of, the network, servers, virtualization, and storage you need. In this scenario, the provider does the datacentre management tasks for you, on your command - for example using an API or management dashboard. IaaS tends to be a cheaper option that allows you to scale up and down quickly as needed. For example, during the software development lifecycle you suddenly realise a need for a new environment. With an IaaS solution you get the servers and spin it up very quickly without the need to purchase new hardware. Public cloud providers such as AWS, Microsoft Azure, and Google Cloud are all examples of IaaS providers.

Platform-as-a-service, or **PaaS** is another step further from on-premises infrastructure management. In this scenario, the service provider hosts the hardware and software on its own infrastructure and delivers this combined platform to you as an integrated solution, over the Internet. Solutions like this are popular among software developers, as they allow them to develop and manage an application their own way without the need to worry about building and maintaining the infrastructure, saving the trouble of hardware maintenance and software updates. The developers can focus on development (coding, building, and managing the applications they own); all environment setup and maintenance is outsourced to the provider. Google App Engine, AWS Elastic Beanstalk, and Heroku are some examples of PaaS solution providers.

Finally, **Software-as-a-service (SaaS)** is the most comprehensive form of cloud computing services. SaaS delivers an entire application via the Internet, so the organisation does not need to worry about hosting and environments, writing code or implementing features. Software updates, bug fixes, and general software maintenance are handled by the provider. The user just connects to the app (no installation on individual computers required) and uses it.

Office365, Gmail, Salesforce, Shopify, etc. are all examples of SaaS providers. Netflix is another example. All these companies are giving you as a user a feature rich application fully available over the Internet (for a subscription fee).

SaaS is a great option for small businesses who don't want to, or simply can't, invest into their own IT team and set of solutions. It is also an option for businesses of any size to outsource the non-unique and repeatable parts of the business, so the internal team can focus on business critical and unique systems; while standard things such as office applications, email, HR processes, etc. are delivered by a service provider. While SaaS saves time and maintenance effort, it does take away a level of control over the applications; that is why companies tend to keep business-critical solutions in-house.

Lesson 25: Data analysis

In IT, we deal with data for transactional purposes all the time: especially when storing details of individual operations. But the same data can also be used to analyse trends and get insights into the business. This is what we call data analysis, or data analytics.

> **Data Analysis** or **Analytics** is the process of systematically applying statistical and/or logical techniques to describe, illustrate and evaluate data. Data analytics is often a prerequisite to implementing Business Intelligence (BI) solutions. **Business intelligence** is a practice and a collection of software solutions that ingest business data and present it in user-friendly views such as reports, dashboards, charts and graphs for ease of consumption by decision makers.

We perform data analysis with the goal of discovering useful information, suggesting conclusions, and supporting decision-making in the organisation.

Depending on the objective, we can distinguish four types of data analysis:

1. **Descriptive**. It answers the question of what has happened. This type of analysis focuses on describing the data in a way that makes it easier to understand for stakeholders. The creation of descriptive dashboards or reports are the usual tasks of descriptive analysis. It

often involves charting and other visualisation tools as well as the means to summarise data.

2. **Diagnostic**. This type of data analysis focuses on why something happened. It analyses potential causes of past events and suggests reasons for what has occurred. Diagnostic data analysis may involve some specialised statistical analysis to identify cause and effect relationships in datasets.

3. **Predictive**. This type of data analysis takes diagnostic analysis to the next level and focuses on the future. It tries to predict what is likely to happen based on an analysis of previous trends and other factors. This is where analysis becomes very technical, taking advantage of complex statistical and mathematical models that allow you to make predictions.

4. **Prescriptive**. This is the most advanced type of analysis. It focuses on advising what the best course of action should be given the known situation. Prescriptive analysis not only tries to predict the future, but focuses on selecting and recommending actions that are most likely to result in desirable outcomes.

Regardless of the type of analysis, to manage an analytics project you are very likely to go through the following steps:

1. **Ask a question**. Analysis starts with formulating a research question to be answered using data as a source. It is important to ensure the question is well defined and understood by all of the participants of the analytics project. Otherwise, you may be answering a question nobody asked, or using data not relevant to what you are trying to uncover.

2. **Source data**. Finding reliable sources of data to answer the question may be a tricky process. Often businesses have massive amounts of unstructured data that is hard to analyse; with some data banks being outdated or inconsistent. Finding data that is reliable enough to base your analysis on is crucial. There is a saying in the analytics world: "Garbage in - garbage out". This means that if you base your analysis on bad data, the result will never be useful.

3. **Extract and prepare data**. Often the way data is stored means it is not ready to be analysed. It requires some initial transformation and preparation. During this step, you obtain the data from the source, perform initial cleansing and then prepare it for analysis. Obtaining data means making it available for your analytics solution to use. For example, you may want to take a data snapshot from the system it sits in and move it to a separate analytics environment due to performance or security considerations. You don't want your analytics algorithms to slow down production systems or accidentally corrupt production data. This step also includes steps to access the data, including technical tasks (e.g., setting up accounts, credentials, and APIs) as well as organisational steps (e.g., get clearance, sign NDA forms, etc.). Once the data is obtained, it needs to be checked for consistency, and reliability. You also need to ensure it is in the format you need. Any issues your encounter along the way should be resolved before you move on to the next step.

4. **Perform analysis**. Once the data is obtained and prepared, you can apply statistical methods to answer the question asked. Usually there will be a data analyst, data scientist or statistician on the team in charge of the actual analysis activities.

5. **Test the results**. Once the analysis is performed, it needs to be validated. You can apply a level of quality control to ensure the results are reliable and free of errors. It may include having some sample or test data sets used only for quality control that are curated in a way which results in expected outcomes after analysis. If the algorithms return the expected results on the test datasets, you may be more confident they will do the same for the real data.

6. **Interpret and present the results**. Finally, getting the results of analysis is one thing, but making sure they are properly used and interpreted is another. You need to prepare the results in a way that can be consumed by the stakeholders. Often this means interpreting what the results mean in terms of answering the original question, and in a business context.

Many businesses understand the power of analytics and decide to implement specialist solutions to enable it.

Often this involves separating the transactional systems (systems that execute business processes and generate data) from the reporting and analysis systems.

This takes care of steps 2 and 3 of the process above. Reliable data sources are identified enterprise-wide and are made available to analytics solutions; this way, when a stakeholder or analyst has a research question, they can jump straight to analysis and play with data, therefore bypassing the step of technically connecting the systems.

A solution that connects multiple data sources and allows real time analysis of that data is called a **data warehouse**.

A **data warehouse** is a type of data management system designed to enable and support business analytics. Data warehouses tend to accumulate large amounts of historical data.

At the core of a data warehouse is a database (often relational). It is supplied with an extraction, loading and transformation mechanism (called ELT) that helps connect external data sources and loads that data into the format expected by the warehouse.

On top of this set up, you will have tools for statistical analysis, reporting and visualisation.

Data warehousing is often discussed together with the concept of **OLAP** (Online analytical processing). OLAP is a software technology and approach to data management that has a data warehouse at its centre, and is designed in a way that allows it to easily combine and group data into categories. This helps provide actionable insights for strategic planning and analysis trends.

The most common data architecture to support OLAP is called star, or the **star scheme**. It consists of a central data table (called "facts table") and multiple dimension tables (tables with extra descriptive information about the facts). The fact table is a data table that contains values related to a transaction or business process. The dimension table contains values that describe each attribute from the fact table. It is one of those concepts that is easier to show than to explain, so let's have a look at an example.

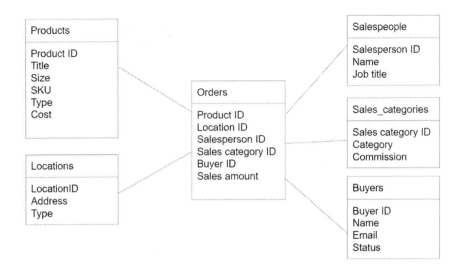

Figure 21. Example of a star shaped data warehouse structure

At the centre we've got a table with Orders data, or a lot of IDs for items participating in that transaction. All the details for those orders are stored in corresponding tables linked to the central one. The table remotely resembles a star shape, thus the name.

This method allows you to easily "slice" the data by one or many of these dimensions. For example, you can see all sales made by a particular salesperson in a particular location, or all of the orders from a particular user (or multiple users) of a particular sales category, and so on. To do this, you just filter the main table by certain IDs (or rather query it by those IDs using SQL).

Data warehousing is not the only way to consolidate data in the business. There are other approaches, such as:
- **Data Lake**: A way to collect data for potential future use. The main difference between a data lake and a data warehouse is that a data lake

does not structure the data to a unified format. It is a great way to store unstructured data such as alerts, social media posts, emails, word documents, etc.

- **Data Mart**: A data mart is similar to a data warehouse, but it serves a specialised function. While a data warehouse collects massive amounts of data for multiple analytical purposes, a data mart is created with a particular stakeholder and their needs in mind. You may end up with multiple data marts, e.g., one for the marketing team, one for the operations team, etc. Each one of the data marts will only contain the data immediately needed by the corresponding team, and nothing extra. This makes data marts easier to implement but may result in duplication or inconsistency of data.

- **Operational data stores** (ODSs): Unlike data warehouses, ODSs support the daily operations of the business, so only store the latest information; their view of historical data is very limited by design.

Useful links for section 5

1. **Cloud Computing Basics: A Non-Technical Introduction**, by **Anders Lisdorf**
   This book offers an introduction to the basics of cloud computing and all major cloud platforms. In non-technical terms it introduces fundamental cloud vocabulary, explains the economic and security benefits of the cloud and explains how to tailor a cloud solution.
2. **Storytelling with Data: A Data Visualization Guide for Business Professionals**, by **Cole Nussbaumer Knaflic**
   This book teaches the fundamentals of data visualisation and how to communicate effectively with data.
3. **Principles of Data Management**, by **Keith Gordon**
   This book is about having the policies and procedures in place within an enterprise so that the various systems can provide high-quality information to their users, even if that information did not originate in the information system with which the user is currently interacting.
4. **SQL All-In-One For Dummies**, by **Allen G. Taylor**
   Just like any book from the *Dummies* series, this one gives a nice overview of the topic and the foundational knowledge to start applying it from day one. If you want to learn SQL, start here.
5. **Database Design for Mere Mortals®: A Hands-on Guide to Relational Database Design**, by **Michael J. Hernandez**
   The book is written in a way that makes complex ideas easier to understand; it's a great introduction to database design.
6. https://medium.com/@jonathanmines/its-all-1s-and-0s-how-computers-map-the-physical-world-18a361fae3a5

An article explaining how computers interpret 0s and 1s. It also lists further reading materials to learn more on the topic.

7. **https://en.wikipedia.org/wiki/Metadata**
This is a nice article explaining metadata. As always, make sure to follow the links and read the sources.

8. **https://afterhoursacademic.medium.com/a-case-for-redundant-array-of-inexpensive-disks-raid-a39858972fec**
A nice overview of what RAID is and how it was invented and developed over time.

< this page is intentionally left blank >

Section 6: Cybersecurity

Introduction to cybersecurity

Security at rest

Authorisation

Security in transit

< this page is intentionally left blank >

Lesson 25: Introduction to cybersecurity

By its very definition, information technology deals with information. However, information has power. Think about it: your passport and birth certificate numbers are stored as information in some government systems; your tax number is stored with your employer; your name and address are stored with every online store you've shopped with. Your recurring payments (the amount of money and who to send it to) is stored with your bank; and all of this is information. If someone with malicious intent gets their hands on it, you may get in a lot of trouble.

It is the job of **cybersecurity** to protect this information, and all of the real assets associated with it. The widespread use of technology and the Internet makes our lives easier, but also introduces risks that humanity has not seen before. IT has become an integral part of our lives, with people relying on it for communication, information sharing, financial transactions, and more. Unfortunately, it has also opened the door to cyber criminals. Cybersecurity is essential because we live in a digital age.

The cyber landscape is changing rapidly. It is not enough to just build an IT solution that works. It needs to have a means of protection against malicious intent and accidental damage. The IT department and infrastructure play an important role in protecting against accidental leaks of information, cyber-attacks, and cyber espionage.

The biggest difference between an **attack** and **espionage** is that the primary goal of a cyber-attack is to disrupt activities or cause damage (often financial), while the primary goal of cyber espionage is for the attacker to remain hidden for as long as possible in order to gather maximum intelligence and use this information to gain a competitive edge.

According to a definition by NIST (the US National Institute of Standards and Technology), Cybersecurity is the protection of information systems from unauthorised activities in order to provide confidentiality, integrity and availability.

Those three terms are the crucial pillars for cybersecurity, they even have their own name: "**the CIA Triad**":

1. Confidentiality
2. Integrity
3. Availability

Let's discuss them in more detail.

Confidentiality is all about keeping data private. This is probably the most natural aspect of security which comes to mind when talking about cybersecurity. You want to protect the data from unauthorised access (access without permission). For example, you don't want the personal details of your customers to become available on the darknet, or the financial statements of your company to become available to the public.

A **dark net** or **darknet** is a hidden network within the Internet that can only be accessed with the help of specialised software and configurations, often via the use of a unique customised communication protocol. Although the darknet is not illegal per se, the way it makes any activity encrypted and anonymised makes it a popular communication and transaction mechanism among cyber criminals. If someone is selling illegal stuff on the Internet (e.g., stolen personal data) they would prefer to do it via an anonymous network, so they don't get caught too easily.

Everyone wants to protect their trade secrets and intellectual property. If you work for the government, you want to protect classified information, and so on. Confidential information, when obtained by third parties, can lead to serious consequences such as identity theft or financial fraud. Failure to protect the personal information of an organisation's clients can lead to regulatory action and even be classified as a criminal offence (depending on the local jurisdiction). Moreover, any issues with data confidentiality can often lead to reputational damage.

There are multiple ways you can ensure data confidentiality, such as by using encryption, implementing access control, and data masking. Encryption involves converting data into an unreadable format, so it is only accessible to authorised people. Access control involves limiting access to sensitive data to authorised people or systems only. Data masking involves altering the data to conceal or obfuscate sensitive information (e.g., when stars replace the last 4 digits of your credit card number on a financial statement).

Integrity is about the ability to keep information in the same state as you left it. Imagine you leave a note for yourself to send a report to management to help them with their decision making on the 10th of May. You rely on this note to not forget about the task. What if someone changed the information on your note without letting you know; let's say they make the date the 12th of May instead. As a result, the report is late, and the decisions are made without the latest information available. It is a simple but relatable example of compromising the integrity of data. More complex ones involve making unauthorised changes to complex data, e.g., financial statements or transactional data.

In general, data integrity ensures that information remains unaltered, complete, correct, and consistent. Data integrity is crucial for decision-making, reporting, and other critical business operations. Data integrity is often demanded by regulations (e.g., when a company is required, by law, to keep records of operations for a certain number of years).

Ensuring integrity involves measures like data validation (formal testing of data quality), error detection (searching for anomalies in data), and data backup (storing immutable data snapshots that can be recovered if needed).

Finally, **availability** is about having access to your data when you need it. Sometimes a lack of availability means you completely lose your data. For example, if a hacker deletes your data from your storage facility. However, availability issues can also be temporary, e.g., making a service unavailable during the time it is needed the most. Data availability is critical for ensuring business continuity and preventing downtime that can lead to financial losses and reputational damage.

Business continuity is an organisation's readiness to maintain critical functions after an emergency or disruption, for example after a security breach, natural disaster, or power outage. Having backup power generators on site and maintaining printed/hand filled logs are some examples of ensuring business continuity in the event of a technical issue.

To better understand how the CIA triad works, let's have a look at a few almost classic scenarios. There is a longstanding tradition to describe these examples using two actors named Alice and Bob and seeing how they communicate with each other.

Let's imagine Alice invites Bob to meet her in a café. Bob agrees, and Alice sends him a message later in the day confirming the time: 10am, tomorrow.

Now imagine there is a third person, Trudy, who likes to intrude into others' lives. What can she do if she gets her hands on this message, and which aspects of CIA will be violated?

Scenario 1: Trudy reads the message and now knows when and where Alice and Bob will meet. This will violate their confidentiality: the message is no longer confidential if it is known to anyone who is not the intended recipient or author of the message.

Scenario 2: Trudy sees the message before Bob can read it, and deletes it, violating the availability of the message. Now Bob will never know where to meet Alice. If Trudy managed to read the message before destroying it, then both the availability and confidentiality of the message are affected.

Scenario 3: Trudy intercepts the message and then changes the time or address of the meeting before Bob sees it. Obviously, the integrity of the message will be affected (Bob will not meet Alice because he will wait for her at the wrong place or time); but also, the message's confidentiality is violated.

Replace Alice and Bob with employees or business entities, a casual catch up in a cafe with a business-critical contract, and Trudy with a hacker - and you will get a grim picture of how much trouble and damage a successful cyberattack can cause.

Lesson 26: Security at rest

When it comes to any data, there are two conceptual points in time when it can be attacked: when it resides, or is stored, waiting to be used (or **at rest**); and while it is transmitted from one storage area to another (or **in transit**).

When data is at rest it sits around waiting to be consumed by a legitimate service. For example, your work files that are stored on your laptop. They sit there waiting for you to open them when you need them. Outside of this time, nothing happens to the files, they are just stored. However, these files need to be protected from being accessed by someone else. Imagine an intruder gets access to your laptop. If this happens, you don't want them to be able to read your files. How do you do that?

Arguably, **encryption** is the best form of protection for data at rest; it's certainly one of the best. You can encrypt files either before storing them or by encrypting the entirety of a given storage drive or device.

Encryption is a way of scrambling data so that only authorised parties can understand the information. In technical terms, it is the process of converting human-readable plain text to incomprehensible text, also known as ciphertext. In simpler terms, encryption takes readable data and alters it so that it appears random. Such data will be of no use to intruders even if they get access to it.

```
All the world's a stage,
And all the men and women merely players;
They have their exits and their entrances,
And one man in his time plays many parts,
His acts being seven ages. At first, the infant.
```
Human readable (Plaintext)

```
s4WH8gRJboEJ1YYIb0kLMnkWAIn1zw/XMVDSWUGihd8VDCrV
QNI/xtQuTmv9Wi3NkOz1zryvXDtfJmFPszHdsLK9jdXYBEZW
1VgJLcTRxAKiNb+sAd4Fn+Zf8+Fuj8QU+NKeXcKLMHBs+GYX
82mN0P+rkfz7FxYh2Wf9yV0j2An2GfZJEWKwX3eiYR+MhXgB
cTur2/iAoL456dNSNW8oafQKJ2MI6iK57GGe2KgbYiCH09Gt
YTOyQSAGCxqIYqkLv3/nvD++0qJS51pd4cdx0juQ9P01A8mj
bCvIrMSHYsM=
```
Incomprehensible (Ciphertext)

Figure 22. An example of encryption. Human readable text gets converted into ciphertext.

Other methods of protecting the data at rest include **access control** via restricting who can get access to data using a means of authentication (we will talk about this in more detail in the next lesson).

Another important aspect of protection is to install **antivirus software** to prevent unauthorised activities on the machine hosting the data.

Antivirus software is a computer program used to prevent, detect, and remove malware. Antivirus software was originally developed to detect and remove computer viruses - self-replicating computer programs that spread computer to computer and often have malicious functionality, such as destroying files, logging user actions, stealing data, or giving access to unauthorised parties. Modern antivirus tools use a combination of antivirus protection as well as network monitoring, anomaly detection, spam filtering and firewall solutions.

A **Firewall** is a network security system that monitors and controls incoming and outgoing network traffic based on predetermined security rules. For example, unknown applications are not allowed to connect to the internet or send data to a given system.

Finally, you can employ a means to recover after a successful attack on your data. It won't save you from confidentiality violations, but it will help in the case of loss of, or modification to, the data. You may store backups of data in different places to reduce the chance of losing backups together with the original data.

When building products or new technology solutions, we should consider how we are going to protect any data generated or acquired by the solution. As you can see, protection means are numerous and sometimes costly or require a lot of effort to set up and maintain. To optimise your security budgets and resources, it is a good idea to categorise the data so that you know what is most sensitive and requires more protection, and what needs less attention. This will allow you to concentrate on the right things and not waste resources.

For example, you may introduce a 3-level categorisation: high-risk data (everything concerning personal information of your customers), medium-risk data (data about your organisation's trading operations or trade secrets), low-risk data (administrative data). You can come up with any categorisation, as long as it helps identify risky data and assets and helps focus the security effort accordingly.

Lesson 27: Authorisation

In the previous lesson we've come across the concept of authorisation. So, what is it?

Authorisation is a multi-step process of making sure that only legitimate users have access to data or functions. Generally, it is a three-step process. When you log in to any application or service, you go through the same three-step process, with some variations for extra security.

The first step is **identification**. At this step a user who is unknown to the system identifies themselves. Typically, a user will do it by stating their account name, email address or other system specified form of ID. In the physical world, when you come to a business office for a service, you would start with saying your name to identify yourself. It is the same in the digital world - the user needs to identify who they are in terms known to the system they interact with.

The next step is **authentication**. This is when you prove that you are indeed the person that you claim to be. To do so you can show evidence of possessing something that only you can have or knowing something that only you can know. This is usually enough to prove that you are in fact you.

Authentication mechanisms check one or a combination of **knowledge** (something only the real user knows), **possession** (something only the real user has), and **inherence** (something only the real user is). Examples could be:
- Knowledge: knowing a secret password or the answer to a secret question

- Possession: having access to a security token, or having access to a particular device
- Inherence: being able to pass face recognition, fingerprint or voice recognition checks

The most typical form of authentication is a password. Because you set your password yourself, if you can present the same password later, then chances are you are the same person. Authentication methods can often be something else, e.g., your fingerprints or facial image. In many cases, especially when dealing with sensitive information, using a password alone is not enough. A password can be stolen, or a hacker can guess the password if it is not secure enough. In this case, a password check will be accompanied by another source of authentication. It may be in the form of answering a secret question that only the user may know the answer to, or confirming the sign-on attempt on another device. This is done to ensure it is in fact you and not someone who just happened to discover your password.

Multi-factor authentication is an electronic authentication method in which a user is granted access to an application only after successfully presenting two or more pieces of evidence to an authentication mechanism. You may see it when you try to log in to your corporate network or get access to your email account, and after successfully using the password you then need to confirm it is in fact you by pressing a button on your mobile device or entering a code from a text message you are sent.

Finally, once the system knows you are you, it **authorises** you to perform certain actions.

As an authenticated user you will be given access to the data and functions permitted by your system role. An operator will have different access rights compared to a manager or an administrator. Once you are authenticated, the system knows who you are. Therefore, it can ensure you only access the data and actions that are allowed to you.

Authorisation mechanisms work in a similar way for human or system actors. If two systems are to exchange information or otherwise communicate (for example via an API) they need to know they can trust each other. A system will go through similar checks:

1. Identification (do I know you?)
2. Authentication (can I trust it is you?)
3. Authorisation (are you allowed to do what you are trying to do?)

Lesson 28: Security in transit

So far, we have discussed securing data at rest and authorising the right users to the right actions. The next vulnerable point occurs when two actors are transmitting the data. While in transmission, the data is exposed to the outside world (the communication channel) and can be intercepted or tampered with.

Imagine you are sending a letter to your friend. While the letter is at your home it is safe. When the letter is received by a friend, it is also safe. And, if the post office workers are trustworthy, the letter will be received in the same state - it will be safe while being delivered. However, if there is a hacker in disguise among the workers, your letter can be compromised when it is being processed at a postal facility, and you will never know.

This process works the same in the digital world. While a piece of data resides in a protected environment, you can rest assured it is fine. But once you need to send it to someone else, this piece of data starts to travel through networks and network devices around the globe. There is no way you can secure them all or trust other parties to secure their devices. So, how can you protect yourself (and your data)?

First of all, encryption is a big helper here.

Unencrypted data, when transmitted, is basically open for anyone to pick up and use. The parties participating in the transaction need ways to ensure the data can be received by the intended recipient; and by them only.

To do so, the participants use special keys to encrypt the messages. Let's get back to our example of Alice and Bob.

If Alice sends a parcel to Bob, she can put her message inside a locked container. To open this container, Bob needs to have the same type of key that Alice used. If she manages to send him the key separately from the container, she can be confident that Bob will be the only person able to open the lock on the container.

The same thing works for digital messages. Say, instead of sending a parcel, Alice wants to send a digital message to Bob, but securely, so she encrypts the data. For Bob to read the data, he needs to know the encryption method used and have a secret key to "unlock" the encryption, allowing him to retrieve the original message from the ciphertext.

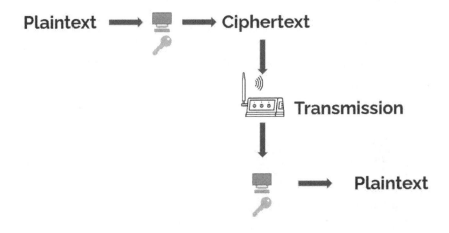

Figure 23. This is how symmetric encryption works. Plaintext is converted into ciphertext before transmission using a secret key. The same key is used to cover the message back to plaintext.

But there is a problem with this method, Alice needs to share her secret key with Bob prior to the transition and she has to do it via a different means for security purposes; i.e. you don't want your lock and the key to open the lock to be sent together. If this happens, a hacker can easily use the key. If she manages to securely share a copy of her key with Bob, she can then use it to encrypt the data and she can be confident that only Bob can read it using his copy.

> This is how **symmetric encryption** works. The same secret key helps to both encrypt and decrypt the data. It works perfectly well but has obvious drawbacks. The main one is that the key needs to be transmitted first; and it can be subject to interception just like any other communication.

There is another way of securely transmitting data using encryption, this is called **asymmetric encryption**. In asymmetric encryption, two separate keys are used. The algorithm uses one key to encrypt the data, but the same key can't be used to decrypt it back or make it useful in any way. This means that the key can be easily shared without any precautions, as even in the wrong hands it doesn't let a hacker decrypt your message; this is called an **open key**.

Now Bob can easily share the open key with the whole world, so that anyone wishing to send him a private message can do so; and they can rest assured that only Bob can decrypt it using his paired secret key, which he keeps private.

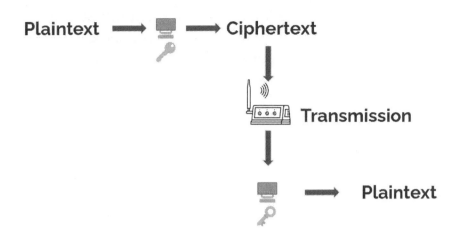

Figure 24. Asymmetric encryption uses different keys for encryption and decryption.

An extra way to keep data secure in transit includes restricting access to data being transmitted. This can be achieved by using firewalls so that only authorised parties can participate in transactions and access the network where the transition is performed. Or it can be done by physically separating the networks – so there is no direct link between different networks at all. It is more expensive, of course, and comes with restrictions, but for more sensitive data it might be worth it.

Finally, an organisation may establish secure connections over the internet that allow it to protect transmitted data. This can be achieved with the help of a VPN.

A **virtual private network** (VPN) is a mechanism for creating a secure connection between a computing device and a computer network, or between two networks, using an insecure communication medium such as the public Internet.

A VPN creates a protected "tunnel" within a network, so any data transmitting within that tunnel is not accessible by any third parties that may have access to the same network. VPNs are often used to allow remote workers access to their work environments, or to connect physically distributed systems.

Useful links for section 6

1. **Cybersecurity For Dummies, by Joseph Steinberg**
   An introductory book to learn the basics of cybersecurity – this will help you to protect a business or your family from cybersecurity threats.
2. **How Cybersecurity Really Works: A Hands-On Guide for Total Beginners, by Sam Grubb**
   Another book that can be used as an introduction to cybersecurity. It teaches all the basics without a lot of jargon and includes a few useful cyber skills.
3. **CompTIA Security+ All-in-One Exam Guide, by Wm. Arthur Conklin, Greg White, Dwayne Williams, Roger L. Davis, Chuck Cothren**
   CompTIA is when things start to get serious. Security+ is one of the industry leading certifications for security professionals, so a book preparing for the exam is a great way to get the full breadth of the profession. It is a very long and technical read, but if learning cybersecurity is your passion this will pay off. This is not the only book that can prepare you for this certification. In my humble opinion, they are all similar, so you can pick any.
4. **https://www.kaspersky.com/resource-center/definitions/encryption**
   An article on encryption published by Kaspersky – one of the leading cybersecurity companies in the world. They have a nice blog and resource hub to help you learn about cybersecurity.
5. **https://www.nist.gov/cyberframework**
   The website for the cybersecurity framework by the National Institute of Standards and Technology in the US. It is a very mature framework that is considered best

practice by the industry, so a lot of organisations are applying it around the globe (and not just in the US).

6. **https://darknetdiaries.com/**

   An amazing podcast about cybersecurity topics. It is more entertaining than educational, but it gives a good sense of the breadth of security concerns of the modern world, and you may learn a thing or two about security while listening to it. I am a fan.

< this page is intentionally left blank >

Section 7: IT management

IT service management

Technical management

Help desk and incident management

IT strategy

< this page is intentionally left blank >

Lesson 29: IT service management

Information technology supports most enterprise activities. Things such as automation, data processing, and connectivity have opened the door to previously unimagined capabilities and efficiencies. Today, business and IT are closely interconnected and can't be easily separated.

At the same time, an organisation is vulnerable when systems underperform or fail. An unresponsive network, lost data or malware can severely impact day-to-day operations.

IT management practices ensure that information technologies are secure, highly available and show the best performance.

IT management is needed to monitor and govern IT systems to ensure they're available and function reliably in line with the expectations of stakeholders.

IT governance is a formal framework that provides a structure for organisations to ensure that IT investments support business objectives.

In other words, IT governance ensures the effective and efficient use of IT in enabling the organisation to achieve its goals.

There is no single definition of what IT management is, but the typical responsibilities and tasks of an IT manager are:

1. Determining business requirements for IT systems
2. Managing IT budgets and costs
3. Monitoring safety and compliance
4. Controlling system and network security
5. Implementing new software, hardware, and data systems
6. Providing technical support

and many more.

Often, an information technology department is perceived as a partner or service provider to business departments. From this point of view, all of the things IT teams do can be described as a series of services provided to the rest of the business so that the business can run.

The approach called **IT Service Management (ITSM)** originates from this idea. ITSM includes elements such as technologies and technical solutions, as well as the processes and people involved in delivering IT services. But the first step is always to define which services are in the scope of your ITSM.

ITSM starts with identifying a finite list of services that are provided by IT to the broader organisation and by defining key performance and success metrics for those services. It is a simple idea: to manage something, you need to have ways to make it visible. This defines the scope of expectations that the organisation will have for the IT department and helps measure the overall performance of IT through its individual services.

It has probably become very theoretical by this point, so let's illustrate it with an example.

If you've got an online shop, then some of the services would be:

1. Website provisioning
2. Product catalogue management

3. Ecommerce processing
4. Order management
5. Delivery management
6. Financial reconciliation
7. Etc.

Each one of those services is a collection of IT systems, processes and people, all of which are focused on delivering a specific outcome for the business.

These are so-called **business services** - services directly consumed by business stakeholders or end users. These stakeholders, due to the nature of their work, will have specific requirements and expectations for the services offered.

The full list of such business services is called a **business services catalogue**. It is usually stored within an IT system, so any interested and authorised person can see the full list and the details of each item within it.

First, they will have functional requirements for the IT solutions behind the services. These will dictate which functionality a service should have (we have covered requirements development in lesson 11).

However, that is not all. Once the solution is built and starts functioning, the non-functional requirements become more prominent. For instance, the financial reconciliation process must be completed in less than 24 hours, otherwise the daily reporting will lag behind; website provisioning should be up and running 24x7 with minimum interruptions, otherwise customers can't place their orders; etc.

Such requirements to the quality of service are collected and agreed with key stakeholders in a formal contract called an SLA (service-level agreement).

A **service-level agreement** (SLA) defines the level of service expected from a vendor, defining the metrics by which service quality is measured, as well as remedies or penalties should service levels be breached.

A SLA can exist between different organisations (usually captured in a vendor contract) or between departments within one organisation (generally defined in policy or other internal regulatory documents).

Each SLA will define how well the service is expected to operate to support the business in a feasible cost-effective manner. It will cover items such as the expected availability of the service, if it is OK to shut it down for maintenance every couple of months, how fast it should work, how fast any identified issues should be responded to and resolved, and so on. The definition of an SLA is usually a trade-off between performance and cost. While it is possible to create services that have no downtime and perform at lightning speed, it will cost a fortune. Decisions need to be made how much performance is enough for the smooth operation of a business, and how much money the organisation is willing to pay for it. If budgets are small, performance sacrifices must be made.

Once SLAs are defined, the organisation can base its public commitments on them. A company can never promise its customers a service better than the underlying SLAs supporting that service.

For a business service to achieve SLA targets it will be supported by a set of technical services. For example, "website provisioning" will depend on a set of underlying services such as: hosting, content management and a content delivery framework, authentication services, security certificates services, and potentially many others. These form a **technical catalogue** - a list of more specific technical services that are not directly or individually consumed by the business users. Instead, they support a business service (or multiple services).

To summarise, the technology division supports business services via delivering technical services.

* * *

Service catalogues must be up-to-date and relevant for the business (otherwise the IT division does not do its job well). To do this the IT team has the power to update, replace or retire technical services when they are no longer fit for purpose.

This service lifecycle management is governed by industry best practices. The **Information Technology Infrastructure Library** (**ITIL**) is a best practices framework for ITSM used by organisations worldwide. The most recent version of ITIL (version 4) emphasizes a collaborative approach to managing IT that breaks down department silos to maintain an agile, flexible IT organisation.

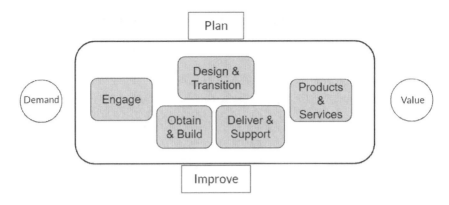

Figure 25. A summary of ITSM and its core processes.

ITIL 4 introduces a six-process service management framework. These processes are:

1. **Plan:** IT services need to be planned considering the business demand, user needs, organisational constraints and overall IT strategy. Through strategic planning the organisation decides which services to retire, to retain, to enhance and to introduce for the first time.

2. **Engage:** To ensure success, IT provider needs to understand the needs of all stakeholders. This activity involves taking a deep dive into user experience needs to keep users satisfied with new IT services.

3. **Design and transition**: Before implementing new services, users' future interactions with the services need to be understood. It is done through user-centric solution design. Decisions are based on stakeholder expectations and organisational strategy.

4. **Obtain and build:** Organisations can develop a new service in-house or purchase a solution from a vendor, depending on user needs and available technologies. This stage is when it happens.

5. **Deliver and support:** After solutions are built or obtained, they are deployed into the IT environment and made available to users. People and processes will require support from IT to make effective use of services.

Changes to organisational structures, working instructions or user manuals may be needed. This is the task for organisational change management: to understand the scope of change in the business and help implement that change.

6. **Improve:** No IT system is simply finished and complete. Effectively managing IT services requires a commitment to continuous improvement, which in turn requires a working feedback channel for the end users to share their issues, concerns, and ideas for improvement.

User-centred design is a process for designing solutions based upon an explicit understanding of users and their tasks in real environments. Instead of designing an ideal interaction with the system in a laboratory environment, user-centred designers study the real context in which users are going to interact with the solutions. This allows them to address the whole user experience and design solutions that are more fit-for-purpose. The process involves real users and their feedback throughout the design and development phases, and it is iterative.

Lesson 30: IT Inventory management

If we get from the strategic level all the way down to individual computers and switches, we will also notice a need for management. Every technology component that the organisation owns needs to be managed. This includes introducing governance to how different components are catalogued and updated over time. You don't want to run an organisation that does not know how many servers it has, or which software licenses it's got, or how much it pays for it all every month.

To solve these managerial challenges, people decided to introduce a catalogue system, or a registry of all technology products, along with which versions or configurations of the product are included, and how those are allocated to users, clients, and other systems.

The resulting registry is often called a **Configuration Management Database (CMDB)**. It is a database of a certain format that stores a record of any **configuration item** in the business.

A configuration item can be anything from monitors and computer keyboards to software products and licenses to infrastructure elements used or owned by the business.

The bigger the organisation, the larger the need to manage configuration items in a consistent manner.

For each configuration item, you are likely to record some metadata. The metadata explains what the item is and what the specifics are for its configuration. You are likely to have different metadata attributes for different types of items. For example, for a physical component you'll have a unique ID of the component, where the component is physically deployed, who the manufacturer is, its serial number, when the last maintenance audit for the component occurred, and who owns it, etc. For a software component it may be where it is deployed and hosted, its IP address, the version of the software, the current license agreement to use it, the patching and maintenance schedule, etc.

This way you've got a structural picture and model of the technology landscape, and you've got a place that will record all the changes to that landscape.

However, it will only be useful if it is updated properly. The moment the CMDB becomes outdated, it loses its value. That is why it is crucial for IT project management and IT change management processes to be integrated into configuration management – so the records of configuration items are always reflective of the real state of object.

Lesson 31: Service desk and incident management

When you have multiple users supported by an IT division, they will have questions, problems, and demands. An organisation needs a way to process those in an organised manner; so that attention is given to requests based on their urgency and competent specialists are assigned to the task. Often it is resolved through a **help desk** function.

A **help desk** or a **service desk** is a centralised team within a company that helps employees or customers with IT related requests.

Service desk staff provide technical support to end users, troubleshoot customer and user issues, and/or guide them through specific tasks and actions; when help desk can't resolve an issue it is their job to find a person or team who can provide the customer with a resolution instead.

Typically, a service desk operates using a specialised software product to manage requests and conversations with customers and users.

Although there is some difference between the two terms – service and help desk – and they do have different origins, today the two are mostly used interchangeably.

The core idea of a service desk is to have a unified entry point where any IT related requests can come through.

A new team member is joining the team and they need a workstation and access to systems? Go to service desk. Your laptop is not performing well, and you need an update? Go to service desk. The website is down, and users can't access it? Go to service desk. You get the gist.

The role of a service desk is to categorise requests based on type and priority and get them resolved in accordance with a specific process designed for the combination of those two.

Examples of types of requests could be:

1. **Standard change**: A simple pre-approved change that can be easily performed by help desk staff. For example, to replace a broken headset, or give access to a particular system.
2. **Change request**: A more complex request for a change in the IT landscape. Something like implementing a new feature or procuring a new license can be categorised as a change request. These types of requests will usually go through an approval process before being actioned and will be supplied with a proper project plan and often be managed as a project. In a project management capacity, you are likely to work with what is considered change requests from the ITSM perspective (not to be confused with change requests to project scope, which is something you might be familiar with).
3. **Service request**: A request to perform some operations within an existing technical landscape without introducing change to the landscape itself. An example could be to create a report, or to deliver a training session, or to collect logs.

4. **Incident report**: A report of an issue with a service. An incident is raised when something doesn't work as well as it was meant to work. Incidents are usually characterised by severity (how bad is the problem, what is the scale of consequences of it) and impact (how widespread it is - is only one customer affected or does the whole customer base experience the same issue?). Incidents are triaged to confirm the ranking, and then are resolved in the order of criticality.

5. **Major incident**: In the case of severe widespread incidents, the company may decide to employ a major incident process. It is a separate process with higher priority for resolution and more prominent communication channels. It sometimes is referred to as a **crisis management** process. When a major incident is declared, it moves the organisation into a state of crisis until the major incident is resolved. This state allows for special procedures to kick in including overtime work, involving extra resources and consultants, and creating real time updates for key stakeholders. A major incident, when resolved, is usually followed by a post-incident review, a process when an organisation studies the root cause of an incident and how well the resolution process went, with the aim to prevent similar issues in the future and within the incident management process.

Depending on the type of the request and its priority and corresponding SLA target (how quickly the team needs to respond to it based on the contract) the request can go through a different escalation route.

ITSM recognises two types of escalation:

Functional escalation happens when an incident is passed to a team or person best equipped to resolve it based on their skills or systems knowledge, and not their seniority. This is a situation when the resolution team admits it does not have enough knowledge to solve an issue and invites an expert. Functional escalation is also called **horizontal escalation**.

It is a part of a standard request processing; often help desk employees have only basic skills to resolve the majority of simple but popular requests, and they are instructed to escalate more complex cases to specialist teams.

Hierarchical escalation is a different process. It involves a request for help from a more senior team member from the same team. An example can be when a junior engineer can't solve a problem and asks for a senior engineer to help. Or a customer support agent can't resolve the customer's request and a supervisor is invited to solve the issue. This type of escalation is also referred to as a **vertical escalation**.

Most requests to service desks will be generated by people: business users of the applications and IT products. However, some of these can also be generated automatically through a monitoring system.

A monitoring system is a special type of IT application that monitors different events in the IT landscape. It can be one system or a collection of multiple systems with a similar purpose – to constantly audit what is happening in the business and alert the IT function when something seems off.

Examples of events that are monitored include: service availability, data exchange between services, user actions such as log in and log off, etc. When an event is categorised as unusual, it will be escalated as an incident for humans to review. If a website is supposed to be up and running but the monitoring system cannot access it, the system will raise an incident that the website seems down. Or if a user's account is marked as disabled but the user suddenly logs into one of the corporate applications, the monitoring system will raise a security incident for the security team to investigate and resolve.

* * *

For an end user, a service desk is a single entry point and a single unit. But from the inside it has a multi-layered structure. Introducing layers helps to manage horizontal escalations and better route the requests. It also helps to optimise cost, so your most experienced (and best paid) employees solve only the hardest and most complex requests, while more junior team members take care of the rest.

A typical service desk will have up to four conceptual layers (with multiple potential teams on each layer). These layers are often called **Levels** or **Tiers.**

Level 0. Initial request acceptance and dispatching to the right team for resolution. If you have one, a call centre will be the level 0 tier. Often this step can be automated via proper categorisation of the request, so after it is created it is sent straight to the team who can perform the investigation.

Level 1. The first line of support. This level consists of people who are skilled in the technology applications they support and who can perform standard troubleshooting and resolution. Level 0 support sends a request to the corresponding level 1 support based on the type of request. The transition of a request to the team more technically skilled to resolve it is called a functional escalation - as opposed to a hierarchical escalation. This is when an incident is passed to a team or person based on their experience level or seniority within the organisation. It is not uncommon to see Level 1 and Level 0 support combined, so the same people perform initial troubleshooting and escalation to other teams when needed. This depends on the size of the team and the number of requests being handled.

Level 2. The second line of support. This level is referred to as **expert support**. Expert support consists of individuals who are highly skilled in the products they support and who can perform the most complex troubleshooting and resolution, including configuration and administration tasks. This is the highest level of escalation within the support teams, before inviting the product engineers for help.

Level 3. The third level of support, or **engineering support**. This level often consists of the engineers and developers of the product. These are the people who might have created the product in the first place, or at least have access to the source code and can make changes to the application in question. Typically, if an incident is caused by a defect in the product, it will be sent to level 3 for resolution, because it requires a change in the product itself. Some teams decide to combine level 2 and level 3 support, especially in smaller sized businesses. Just like the decision to combine level 0 and level 1, it is based on the size of the team and typical amount and type of requests.

Level 4. The fourth level of support, or **vendor support**. If a product is developed by a third party, it may require their assistance for an incident to be resolved. Typically, what we call level 4 support for our organisation becomes just the first line of support in the corresponding vendor's organisation.

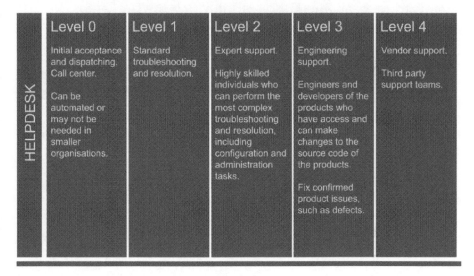

	Level 0	Level 1	Level 2	Level 3	Level 4
HELPDESK	Initial acceptance and dispatching. Call center. Can be automated or may not be needed in smaller organisations.	Standard troubleshooting and resolution.	Expert support. Highly skilled individuals who can perform the most complex troubleshooting and resolution, including configuration and administration tasks.	Engineering support. Engineers and developers of the products who have access and can make changes to the source code of the products. Fix confirmed product issues, such as defects.	Vendor support. Third party support teams.

Figure 26. The four-level service desk structure

The structure above is not a must have, and it can be altered based on the organisation's size and needs. You may see specialised units within the support structure. An example could be a dedicated technical account manager (an expert support team member who assumes the functions of level 0, 1, and 2 for a selected list of priority customers or end users). A technical account manager can be assigned to the most important client business as a part of their support agreement or as a courtesy. A similar person can be nominated to provide direct support to selected employees, e.g., CEO office. Another example could be a special major incident response team – a support team whose job it is to monitor and respond to major incidents only.

Regardless of how the organisation structures its support function, it is important for any newly introduced solutions to be properly transitioned into ongoing support and maintenance. From the IT project management perspective, it is not enough to implement the solution to the specification. It needs to be properly introduced through the IT change management process (with corresponding records in CMDB and following the organisational change management procedures) and it needs to be handed over to the service desk team for support (so they know how to categorise the requests, identify, and troubleshoot likely issues, and know which escalation rules to follow for requests associated with the new product).

Lesson 32: IT strategy

As you can see, information technology consists of many components, which without guidance will likely end up in disarray and chaos. This is where top management plays a role in IT, specifically through an **IT strategy**.

> Technology strategy (information technology strategy or IT strategy) is the overall plan consisting of objectives, principles and tactics relating to the use of technologies within a particular organisation. Such strategies primarily focus on the technologies themselves, but also on people who manage and operate these pieces of tech.

A technology strategy is a document and aligned understanding of how the use of information technology will support the business in achieving its business strategy. Based on the IT strategy, the whole IT architecture will be defined and organised.

Typically, the IT strategy is something owned by the top-level or C-level executive in the IT line of business, such as a CIO (chief information officer) or CTO (chief technology officer).

The IT strategy may consist of two important components:

1. **A capability model**: What technology capabilities the organisation needs to have in order to achieve its goals.
2. **An operating model**: How technology teams will be structured, what types of people needed to support it,

and how responsibilities will be distributed between these people.

A **technical capability** refers to how an organisation can use technology to support and enable the achievement of business goals and objectives. Also known as Technical Reference Architecture.

Software can sometimes be generalized and configured to do different things. Technical capability models allow organisations to spot opportunities to capture missing functionality in the application portfolio, streamlining the software it pays for and maximising IT spend.

Technical capabilities are usually defined without the reference to particular vendors and technology solutions, which come into play later as a part of designing the future state architecture delivering the designed capability.

Some examples of technical capabilities may include software development, data analytics, cloud computing, business intelligence, AI, etc.

For each of them, the IT strategy will define the right approach. It may say, for example, that the strategy for software development is outsourcing to another country; a strategy for AI is to build internal machine learning tools and a talent pool; and that cloud computing will not be used for mission critical systems. Of course, the real IT strategy will be more detailed than this, but I hope it gives you a sense of the types and level of decisions that IT strategy contains.

The process of defining IT strategy will be supported by implementing IT service management and its related aspects (discussed above), Enterprise architecture development (which we touched upon at the very start of the course), and Governance which will measure the maturity of the organisation and its compliance to its own standards and commitments.

Useful links for section 7

1. **ITIL Foundation,** by **AXELOS**
   The Information Technology Infrastructure Library (ITIL) is the collection of best practices for managing IT services.
2. **Implementing World Class IT Strategy: How IT Can Drive Organizational Innovation,** by Peter A. High
   The author describes an importance of having an IT strategy that is aligned with the broader business strategy and not isolated from it.
3. **Staying the course as a CIO: How to overcome the trials and challenges of IT leadership,** by Jonathan Mitchell
   This book is written for IT leaders and those aspiring to be one. It is full of real-world insights about the IT leadership role and explains how to navigate the key challenges of it.

Final notes

I hope you have enjoyed reading this book as much as I have enjoyed writing it. Honestly, I did not trust myself to finish this work when I started, but hey you never know!

This book covered a lot of ground in what I hope was a not too technical introductory style. I did include a lot of links and recommendations for further reading after every section, but this list is by no means comprehensive. There are lots of good books, articles, magazines, and courses out there to get started in the world of IT. I hope that after reading my book you've got enough general knowledge to start a more specialised learning journey or can now decide what you need to focus on. Or it at least helps you answer some of those tricky interview questions.

A lot of the things in the book are based on my own views and experiences. It is ok that some people may have different views, or some organisations may not follow the rules and definitions I have used. The IT industry is very diverse, with a lot of approaches and good practices, which sometimes contradict each other or conflict if implemented together. That is also ok and is a symptom of a fast-growing industry. I'm curious where it will take us in a few decades.

For now, I wish you all the best in starting your IT career. It is an exciting world, where every day brings something new.

Good luck, and let's stay in touch.

Yours,
Igor

About the author

Igor's career started more than a decade ago in the basement of a multi-apartment building where he was a part of an indie internet advertising firm. Since then, he's been a business analyst and a BA team manager in multiple organisations, including a practice manager for BPM in a cybersecurity organisation, a head of business analysis in a consulting firm, and a manager for an agile delivery practice in fintech.

Igor is a founder of Analyst's Corner, an IIBA Endorsed education provider that focuses on liberating the BA education: leveraging peer-learning through a community blog and offering affordable paid options for anyone interested in business analysis.

Since his university days, Igor has been fond of teaching and helping others learn. He delivered a few lectures to first year students during his Master's program and that has ignited the passion. Since then, he's been a regular presenter at industry events, meetups, and webinars; and a guest lecturer at University of Melbourne. He has recorded multiple online courses for business analysts, project managers and agile practitioners. These courses receive high rating and are popular among both newstarters and veterans of the industry.

Index

Made in United States
Troutdale, OR
03/04/2024

18211671R00117